MAKING SENSE OF GOD

To Maureen,
    It was a pleasure to
meet you in Boston + be
part of this conversation with
women. May it continue!

                    Peace
                    Elizabeth Dreyer
                    Sept. 23, 2008

Making Sense of God

A

WOMAN'S

PERSPECTIVE

Elizabeth A. Dreyer

ST. ANTHONY MESSENGER PRESS
Cincinnati, Ohio

Excerpts from Raniero Cantalamessa, *Come, Creator Spirit: Meditations on the* Veni Creator, copyright ©2003 by Order of Saint Benedict, Inc. Published by Liturgical Press, Collegeville, Minnesota. Reprinted with permission.

Excerpts from *The Inclusive Psalms*, copyright ©1997, Priests for Equality, Brentwood, Maryland. Reprinted with permission.

Scripture passages have been taken from *New Revised Standard Version Bible*, copyright ©1989 by the Division of Christian Education of the National Council of the Churches of Christ in the U.S.A., and used by permission. All rights reserved.

Cover and book design: Mark Sullivan
Cover image: www.jupiterimages.com/Plush Studios/Bill Reitzel

LIBRARY OF CONGRESS CATALOGING-IN-PUBLICATION DATA
Dreyer, Elizabeth, 1945-
Making sense of God : a woman's perspective / Elizabeth A. Dreyer.
p. cm. — (Called to holiness : spirituality for Catholic women)
Includes index.
ISBN 978-0-86716-884-6 (pbk. : alk. paper) 1. Catholic women—Religious life. 2. Spirituality—Catholic Church. I. Title.
BX2353.D74 2008
248.8'43—dc22
2008017861

ISBN 978-0-86716-884-6

Published by St. Anthony Messenger Press
28 W. Liberty St.
Cincinnati, OH 45202
www.SAMPBooks.org
www.CalledtoHoliness.org

Printed in the United States of America.

Printed on acid-free paper.

08 09 10 11 12 5 4 3 2 1

I wish to acknowledge the support and encouragement of an organization of philanthropists: Foundations and Donors Interested in Catholic Activities (FADICA). In January of 2005, I was invited to speak before this organization at a conference entitled Women of Faith. The discussion explored the many contributions of women to Roman Catholic ministry, church leadership and theology.

The members of FADICA heard my appeal for a renewed focus on women's spirituality in the context of significant religious change during the twentieth century and the pressing challenges of the twenty-first. The need for a creative, solidly grounded, and theologically sophisticated spirituality available in an accessible form for all Christian women seemed obvious. Follow-up conversations by the FADICA board, ably led by Frank Butler, led to a proposal from Fairfield University for a series of books on women's spirituality. Thus, FADICA, Fairfield University, and St. Anthony Messenger Press formed a collaborative partnership to produce seven volumes under the title *Called to Holiness: Spirituality for Catholic Women.*

I wish to thank individuals and foundations whose generosity made this collaborative venture possible. These include the Amaturo Family Foundation, the AMS Fund, the Cushman Foundation, the Mary J. Donnelly Foundation, George and Marie Doty, Mrs. James Farley, the Robert and Maura Burke Morey Charitable Trust, Maureen O'Leary, Ann Marie Paine and the Raskob Foundation for Catholic Activities. I wish to extend a word of thanks and praise to the entire FADICA membership, whose conscientious, quiet and loving participation in shaping the life of the church has been an inspiration.

I also want to acknowledge the support of Jeffrey von Arx, S.J., president of Fairfield University, and Dr. Timothy Snyder, former dean of arts and sciences, for their encouragement and support. Noel Appel, director of foundation relations at Fairfield University, was involved in the proposal from the beginning and graciously shepherded it through its many stages. I also want to thank my associate editor, Jean Marie Hiesberger, for her wise counsel and insight. Charlene Wallace offered unflagging support and humor, attended to the nuts and bolts of administration and communication, and graciously read and commented on several manuscripts. Robert Heyer and Robert Nicola provided much needed counsel on the contractual elements of this multifaceted project. Lisa Biedenbach, Katie Carroll and the staff at St. Anthony Messenger Press lent their support from start to finish, nurturing the idea of this series and turning manuscripts into books.

I also want to thank friends and colleagues who read drafts of this volume and provided helpful conversation and comments: Barbara Cooke, Bertie James Daw, Anna Kish, Diane Schultz, Deborah Spaide and Leanne Wiedemann. I owe special appreciation to my most loyal and loving friend, critic and editor, John B. Bennett, who is ever-ready to lend an ear, cheer me on, offer his considerable editorial skills and love me into speech these many years.

The focus of this series is spirituality. Its interest is women of all types: rich and poor; married and single; white, black and brown; gay and straight; those who are biological mothers and those who are mothers in other senses. There will be volumes on theology, life stages, family life, prayer, action for justice, youth, wisdom years and Hispanic heritage. I hope all the volumes in this series will deepen and shape your own theology in creative ways, as you engage with the theology of our rich, two-thousand-year-old Christian tradition.

Grassroots theology is done by female Christians in light of their concrete, specific experiences of joy and struggle; ecstasy and despair; virtue and vice; work and leisure; family and friends; embodiment and sexuality; tears and laughter; sickness and health; sistering and mothering. It is done by women and men from all walks of life, whether new to the spiritual journey or old hands, whether affluent, middle-class or poor. It is done by people in every country on the planet, by those who are at the center, the margins or even outside the official circle we call church.

The time is ripe for "ordinary" women to be doing theology. The first and second waves of the women's movement in the nineteenth and twentieth centuries provided a valiant and solid foundation for the third wave which will mark, and be marked by, the world of the early twenty-first century. The changes and developments from one generation to the next seem to have sped up. Younger women readers are likely to be already grooming the soil for a fourth wave of Christian theology done by and for women. Women have always loved God, served others and struggled with sin, but the historical context has been less than friendly in terms of women's dignity, acknowledgement of female gifts and empowerment by church and society. In a time of growing emphasis on the role of clergy, and the backlash against women in society, the voices of the laity—especially the voices of women—are needed more than ever.

The Greek language has two words for time. *Chronos* points to the time signaled by the hands on the clock—for example, it is a quarter past two. *Kairos* points to time that is ripe, a moment pregnant with possibility. As Christian women, we live in a time rightly described as *kairos*. It is a time that calls us, demands of us renewed energy, reflection and commitment to attend to and help each other grow spiritually. At this point in history, the fruit of women's struggle includes new self-awareness, self-confidence and self-respect. More and more women are beginning to see just how lovable and capable they are. The goal of the Christian life has always been to lay down our lives in love for the other, but the particular ways this vocation is lived out differ from era to era and place to place. Women's ability to voice with confidence the phrase, "I am a theologian" at the beginning of the twenty-first century means something it could not have meant even fifty years ago.

Those who were part of the early waves of feminism celebrate the hard-won accomplishments of the women's movement and know that this work needs to be taken up by future generations. Young women in their twenties and thirties are often unaware of past efforts that brought about more dignity and freedom for women. Women have opened many doors, but many remain closed. We must be vigilant and continue to act for decades to come in order to secure our accomplishments thus far and make further inroads toward the creation of a just, egalitarian world. Those who sense that the women's movement is in a doldrums inspire us to renew the enthusiasm and dedication of our foremothers.

When we cast our eye beyond the women of our own nation, it takes but a split second to realize that the majority of the world's poor and oppressed are women. A quick visit to the Women's Human Rights

Watch Web site reveals the breadth and depth of women's oppression across the globe from poverty and domestic abuse to sex slavery. Most women (and their children) do not have enough to eat, a warm, dry place to sleep or access to education. Female babies are more at risk than male babies. Women, more than men, lack the protection of the law and the respect of their communities. The double-standard in sexual matters affects women in harmful ways in all cultures and economic groups across the globe.

For all of these reasons it is not just important—but pressing, crucial, urgent—that all women of faith own the title "theologian" and shape this role in light of each woman's unique set of characteristics, context and relationships. We are theologians when we sort through the great and small problems of our time through reflection on Scripture or the words of a mystic or theologian. The images of God that emerged for Paul, Augustine or Catherine of Siena provide guidance, but their theology cannot ever be a substitute for our own. Theology helps us shape what we think about God, justice, love, the destiny of humanity and the entire universe in a way that is relevant to the specific issues facing us in the twenty-first century.

The spiritual options available to us would make our great-grandmothers' heads spin. In fact, they likely make our own heads spin. Our options range from funky New Age to fundamentalism and every thing in between. In Matthew's Gospel, Jesus counsels his disciples to build their houses on firm foundations (see Matthew 7:24–27). A lively theological foundation can assist us to build our spiritual houses on rock and identify the sandy elements that will not sustain us over the long haul of life's joys and sufferings.

This book invites you to engage in this theological task, to reflect on life in light of faith in the Trinity. The task calls for imagination, intelligence, confidence and commitment. Where is the sand and where is the rock in your spiritual foundation? I suggest that theology is a solid, intelligent and necessary ingredient that will help hold up our spiritual houses as we live from day to day. I invite you to accompany me on a journey that explores what theology is, various ways to do it and how it affects both the mundane and glorious adventures life inevitably brings.

Most people see spirituality as open to everyone—it is a work of the heart. In contrast, theology is usually linked with the head and seen as an esoteric, specialized activity. This book differs from these common assumptions. While what follows underlines the importance of distinctions, the ultimate goal is not to build a wall between spirituality and theology but to keep them together in animated conversation. *Both* spirituality and theology require *both* head and heart. But because we may feel on the inside track when it comes to spirituality and on the margins in the world of theology, we will emphasize the latter and aim to establish a better balance between the two. Why not be an insider in both worlds?

I have vivid memories of learning from my mother—in quiet, indirect ways—the important place of faith in my life as a young woman. In her eyes, not only was being female special, but amazingly, it included reading, studying and talking theology. When I was a sophomore in high school, my mother returned to the profession she had practiced briefly in the late 1920s. She took a job as an eighth-grade teacher in our local parish school. Geography and religion were her favorite subjects. In the evening, after sports and music events, she, my younger sister and I sat at the dining room table and studied. During our nightly tea break, we discussed the geography of the world, Thomas Merton and Hans Küng.

Thus, from an early age I was influenced by the seed she planted—the message that faith and theology were important. Christians do not require formal theological education in order to do theology. Education and intellectual work take many different forms—most are outside the classroom. God gave intelligence to *all* human beings and I think it safe to presume that God would like all of us to use it. Throughout history totalitarian powers have consistently disempowered select social groups by denying education and blocking access to the language and thought patterns necessary to participate in society. It is hard to influence politics, culture, education or religion when we lack the vocabulary and the know-how to engage in conversation about issues central to our well-being. In addition, the world has persistently identified women with the body and feeling, and men with the mind and reason. Within this larger cultural matrix, Christianity has spoken up for women's dignity but also excluded their voices from theology and decision-making.

As one of the most literate cultures in the world, we engage our minds when it comes to work, politics, literature, child-rearing, human development, relationships, even hobbies. In addition to the immense wisdom developed in the vocations of child-rearing, education and healing, women now also grace outer space, boardrooms, university classrooms, research labs, Congress and perhaps soon even the White House. We listen to the news, read, ask questions, compare and contrast, have conversations with family and friends—all in an effort to name, understand and make sense of the world in which we live. When we engage in such activities in the world of spirituality and religion, we are functioning as theologians.

Being a theologian is not an easy task. As women, we need to develop two mind-sets as we approach the tradition. We need to be on our guard (hermeneutics of suspicion); and we need to be creatively open (hermeneutics of embrace). *Hermeneutics* is a term that refers to the art of interpretation. We interpret Scripture, events, experience, doctrines, laws, liturgy and work for justice. In the first mode, we need to view the tradition with a careful eye, since the Christian tradition has had an ambiguous track record toward women. For example, the Scriptures tell us that Mary Magdalene was the first witness to the resurrection (see John 20:11–18). In the early church she was known as "the apostle to the apostles," but for much of Christian history she has been known primarily as a loose woman.

We also know that there are different ways the Christian community has interpreted the story of Adam and Eve. One emphasizes the derivative relationshp of woman to man (as in Genesis 2:21), while the other celebrates their equality (as in Genesis 1:27ff). Who did the interpretation and why was the story interpreted in these particular ways? Who benefited and who was negatively affected by any given interpretation? How do we understand this passage today? When we ask good questions, we make discoveries that allow us to live with a more informed and directed faith.

In the second mode (hermeneutics of embrace), we view the tradition with an open heart. This means that we trust the Bible and Tradition as gifts from God to guide us in our faith journeys. While we must ask hard questions to uncover biases in the tradition, we also accept it as the fruit of the Holy Spirit's power in our midst. We listen with an open mind and heart to the promptings of the Spirit. We pray the Scriptures and reflect on the tradition, trusting that God continues to spcak to us. We open ourselves to the "cloud of witnesses" (Hebrews 12:1) who have lived loving, compassionate, prophetic, faith-filled lives. For example, we allow the story of the Canaanite woman who would not be deterred from asking Jesus for help, to inspire us to perseverance in our prayers for loved ones, our entreaties for a suffering world, and in our struggle for a theological voice (Matthew 15:21–28). Jesus interpreted her refusal to take no for an answer as an act of deep faith.

Spirituality is the journey of falling in love with God and living out that love in everyday life. It might include service to the poor, support of causes that contribute to the common good, spiritual practices, developing a life of virtue. Theology is ordered reflection, in which we interrogate our experiences in order to name and make sense of them from a faith perspective. Where is God in this? Who is the God lurking behind our attitudes, behaviors and prayer? Who are we in the sight of God?

In the chapters to follow, I identify several key themes from a rich smorgasbord of theological ideas. I chose particular topics that I think are important, relevant and pressing at this point in history. I hope conversation about these themes will entice you to further exploration. There is so much to learn, so much to live.

Part one explores the possibility of viewing ourselves as *theologians*. Who, me? No way...or is there a way? I remember the knowing gleam in the eye of one of my students when she discovered that theology was not the exclusive domain of priests and religion professors as she had thought. The energy behind her newfound power was quickening. Chapter two discusses our ability to notice God in the world, or sacramental consciousness. In what ways do we experience an intrinsic holiness of the world—in spite of sin and suffering?

Part two explores the many faces of God, with a special focus on the Holy Spirit. When we think and speak about God, we use qualities and images too numerous to contemplate—multiple ideas built up over a lifetime. God is friend, aunt, father, rock and fortress, mother, feather, eagle. God is compassionate, just, patient, angry, honest, forgiving, steadfast, awesome. Our discussion focuses on how these images are based in the tradition's ideas about God as Trinity—the God who creates, becomes incarnate and makes holy.

Part three examines two practical and sometimes thorny issues for women's spirituality: self-sacrifice (asceticism) and virtue. These chapters are followed by a discussion of the relationship between theology and spirituality, with a comment on what is known as "negative theology." These topics are intended as a source of encouragement and creativity for your theology and spirituality; they may also alert you to how much theology you are already doing.

PART ONE

• GRASSROOTS THEOLOGY •

The tradition teaches us that theology can be done, must be done,
that when it is done, we are confronted with mystery and bow our
heads in adoration.[1]

A basic definition of grassroots theology might go something like this:
Grassroots theology is the prayerful, informed, thoughtful reflection on
our lives locally and globally in light of the loving, challenging presence
of God. Grassroots theology identifies and uses images, metaphors,
words, stories, concepts and categories that point to life lived in partnership with God and each other. Grassroots theology is for everyone
who asks questions and seeks to understand their faith more deeply and
broadly.

Theological reflection begins by asking questions of our life experience. How do our thoughts, values and behaviors align with the wisdom of the tradition to which we have given assent in faith? When our
lives clash with this tradition, we ask why. Do they clash because we do
not want to be challenged by truly striving to live a Christian life, or do
they clash because our consciences are genuinely leading us in other
directions? For example, in North America, many struggle with afflu-
ence and consumerism. How do we live in this culture and remain
faithful to the simplicity and radical love of the gospel? The point is not
to become a rigidly defined cookie cut out of the tradition, but to
embody the deepest truths of that tradition in lively, creative, honest
and faithful ways in a twenty-first–century culture.

We all participate in theological reflection to some extent. In this section of the book, we'll explore what that means for us as women, and what it can mean for the world.

CHAPTER ONE

• THEOLOGICAL IDENTITY •

All of us need to make sense of God, but theology might seem beyond our wondering about life, the universe and our place in it. Let us begin by taking an important first step. Take a couple of deep breaths. Close your eyes and open your mind and heart. Slowly, deliberately, and with a quiet confidence say: "I am a theologian." Pause. Repeat it again. Pause. One more time: "I am a theologian." Now take a moment to notice your reaction to this exercise. Was it new, commonplace, welcome, strange, frightening, exhilarating, puzzling? Were you hesitant, reduced to silence or, by the third iteration were you shouting it to the treetops? Can you explain your reaction? What are the factors that affected the ownership or rejection of your identity as a theologian?

We are calling the type of theology under discussion "grassroots theology." Some of us have never heard of this kind of theology. Others wish there were more recognition and attention paid to it. It is good for the church when ordinary people do theology in thoughtful, prayerful ways. It is important because virtually 99 percent of the active church is made up of laity (and most are women). If theology is to represent the community's experience of faith adequately, we need all our voices. It is likely that many of us do grassroots theology spontaneously every day. Consider the woman who finds herself constantly complaining and criticizing family and colleagues at work. She takes a moment to reflect on the term *eucharist*—a word that means "thanksgiving"—and resolves to interject short words of thanks throughout her day. This links her Sunday worship and her profession of faith with her daily attitudes and speech.

Theology = Theos + Logos = God + Understanding/Meaning

The term *theology* has within it the Greek word for God—*theos*. Thus, to "do theology" means to place God at the center of our reflections on life. Theologians look at the world, and everything and everyone in it, and ask: What has God got to do with all of this? What is the meaning of my life from a godly perspective? For centuries, the Christian tradition has thought of theology as "faith seeking understanding" *(fides quaerens intellectum)*, in other words, making "faith sense" of our lives. One of theology's major jobs is to keep intact the link between God and faith on the one hand, and humanity, history and the universe on the other. We are mindful of the tradition (all the ways in which Christians have lived and spoken about their encounters with God, such as biblical commentary, spirituality, theology, liturgy, art, doctrine and church documents) but also use that tradition in lively, creative ways that make sense in this particular time and place. Tradition is not a museum but an artist's workshop, a continuous process of formation and the creation of new values and experience.

Formal Christian theology is arranged into subdisciplines and these various branches emerge out of, and are accountable to, the lived experiences of the Christian community. First, people have to fall in love with God and choose faith. Then they can reflect on these experiences in an ordered way. In turn, the faith of the community is shaped by theology—a relationship we will explore more fully below. You may have a favorite topic, such as Bible study which is the foundation for all theological reflection. Or you may be drawn especially to the Trinity (the theology of the community of Father/Mother, Son and Spirit), Christology (the study of Christ), pneumatology (theology of the Holy Spirit), ethics, eschatology (the study of the endtimes), Christian anthropology (the study of the human person), or a particular period of history such as the early church, the Middle Ages, or the modern and postmodern periods.

Like our entire world, theology is also pluralistic. There is never only one version. Thus, we need to work at maintaining unity while being open and hospitable to learning about viewpoints that are different from ours. Genuine conversation in which we truly listen to each other with open hearts is one of the greatest challenges of our global existence. We search for ways to articulate and respect the quite different ways in which human beings talk about ultimate meaning. This pluralism can mutually correct and enhance different viewpoints in honest, open conversation. *Not* to know our tradition, *not* to do theology, *not* to engage in reflection about God, is not to realize fully our humanity as God's creatures. In particular, we need to hear more from female believers across the globe.

Since theology arises out of the experience of different groups of believers, the Christian community embraces many perspectives. While all profess faith in a trinitarian God and are committed to be followers of Christ, each group does theology in a distinctive key. Each seeks to understand and live the meaning of Jesus Christ in the context of specific cultures: Orthodox (Greek, Russian); Protestant (Lutheran, Reformed, Congregational, Anglican, Methodist and Amish); Roman Catholic are among these varieties. Additional strains arise out of the experience of more recent evangelical and Pentecostal movements. Some Catholics may be familiar with different forms of monastic theology such as the traditions of the Benedictines, the Franciscans, the Dominicans and the Jesuits. Lay theology has also come into its own in the Roman Catholic Church after Vatican II. Thousands of laypersons (especially women) have received degrees in theology pre-paring them for a wide variety of ministries in the church.

Global communication increases our awareness of grassroots theological movements across the world. Liberation theologies were born out of the experience of oppression in Central and South America. The poor reflected on their suffering and joys in light of the gospel. They turned to the gospel in organized, communal settings, as a source not only for comfort and healing but as a vehicle for discernment and change. They discovered anew that the enormous gap between rich and poor is counter to Jesus' message. This empowered them to speak the truth to unjust power and work for personal, social and economic rights. Other versions of liberation theology include: African American theology, *minjung* theology in Korea and feminist theologies—which are of particular interest to us in light of the goals of this series, *Called to Holiness*. This theological variety reminds us that theology is intensely local as well as universal. We need to ground our theologies in our particular contexts, but we are also responsible to enter into dialogue with those whose experience is different, alien or puzzling to us.

Most of us define theology in a way that conjures an image of solemn, ponderous, ivory-tower (likely male) professors. Let's call this type of theology professional or academic theology. This type of theology can be boring and removed from real life or lively, creative and having everything to do with the most important issues of existence. The latter is an important and much-needed form of academic theology.

Grassroots theology and professional theology are partners, working together to make sense of, find language, images and metaphors for, and assign meaning to, the ways in which God acts in the world and human beings respond. Grassroots theology is a privilege, a calling, a responsibility of every baptized Christian. It involves prayerful, ordered reflection on every aspect of reality in the light of God's creative love, Christ's redeeming presence, and the Holy Spirit's empowering action. In this volume we will refer to professional theology on occasion, but our primary concern is its partner—grassroots theology.

The World of the Twenty-First Century

Before we say more about grassroots theology, we need to pause to say a word about the importance of context in doing theology. All of us do theology in a particular geographic, historical and social context. As a card-carrying, bona-fide citizen of the Western world, do you ever feel like your existence is built on sand? A passing glance backward at the twentieth century generates a collage of conflicting emotions. There have been welcome advances in medicine and education, and the technological and communications revolutions leave my head spinning. The gap between older and younger generations has become a chasm when it comes to computers—at least that is the case at my house. We reel at the rate of change in the span of one short lifetime, but are grateful for changes that have enhanced the dignity of many across the globe who had been relegated to the sidelines—female persons prominent among them.

We are also heirs to an incredibly violent legacy—war, famine, genocide, greed and corruption. Individual and corporate sin fills the headlines. For the first time in history, it has dawned on us that our destructive behaviors are threatening the health of the planet that sustains life for all species. In addition, the pace of our daily lives can shorten our breath and turn reflection into a mirage.

In an American culture growingly ignorant about historical and religious traditions, our spiritualities may be monopolized by individual, personal experience, or even by fads, celebrity culture or media advertising. I am not suggesting that personal experience is not important. It is one of the bedrocks of our spiritual lives. But Christian faith challenges us not to isolate our personal experience from the larger cultural and faith communities. Together, all of our experiences form a tapestry that ideally has God at the center.

We are also confronted with a new dichotomy between being "spiritual" and "religious." For many, the spiritual life has been set adrift from age-old language, symbol systems and rituals. For all its blessings, this more individualized spirituality may not hold up over the long haul of hundreds of years. In what follows, I invite you to reflect, ask questions, and grow in your awareness of the theological underpinnings of your spiritual life. What is your personal theology? What pieces of the tradition have been most meaningful for you as a woman of the twenty-first century? What aspects of the faith are no longer meaningful? While theology is often seen as inaccessible and irrelevant to the person in the pew, it need not be, for it arises out of, and informs, the very fabric of our lives—our personalities, our life experience, our gifts and weaknesses, our relationships with creation, the world, ourselves and God.

Grassroots Theology

As Christians, we view life through a very particular lens—the presence of God, in and through Jesus Christ and the power of the Holy Spirit. Baptism commissions us to be on the lookout for the Word of God in the world. This means first of all attending carefully to the world, drawing back the *veil* (from the Greek root of the word for "mysticism") in order to see more clearly the goodness, truth, beauty and love all around us. We also attend with tears and compassion to suffering and work to alleviate it. Matthew's Gospel about building houses on a solid foundation can refer to the ways theology grounds our spiritual lives, helps us hear the Word of God, hold it in our hearts and try to live it out faithfully (see Matthew 7:24–27).

Thus, theology helps us make deeper sense of our spiritual lives. It makes us more aware of how our spiritualities do or do not relate to the Scriptures, to the stories of those dedicated Christians who have gone before us, to the world around us. Theology fosters knowledge and love of God through careful engagement with the tradition in the context of the world in which we live. For example, some of us may think that Christian spirituality and theology have been exactly the same for two thousand years. To the contrary, the tradition is rich and diverse. Persons very different from ourselves have loved God in their particular historical contexts and through their unique personalities. Theology can help us find a whole company of witnesses to the Good News of the Gospel, discover fresh ways to think about God, grace, humanity and prayer and realize that we are less alone than we thought. In each age we are called, *as women*, to ask questions:

- How, where and when do we experience God?
- What names do we give to God and why? Do these names point to what we need from God?
- How do we imagine God? As a person? As an aspect of the natural world?
- What do we know about the Bible? About Tradition? What would we like to know?
- How do we think God imagines us?
- To what might we liken our relationship with God? What images and metaphors come to mind?
- What are our deepest desires for ourselves, our loved ones, our world?
- What brings us life and freedom in the Spirit?
- What brings slavery and death?

Requirements for doing theology include baptism, paying attention to life with reverence and openness, sheltering a moment or two for reflection, knowing the Christian story, and above all, having a desire to live our faith with intelligence, to love God and neighbor and to work actively toward creating a just and humane world.

Theology invites us to reflect on our lives in terms of their *ultimate* significance. To do theology is to be thoughtful, to reflect on what we want to have in our hands at the end of life's journey. Engaging in theology may lead us to begin each day with a view from our own death beds. What do I want my life to have been about *ultimately*? Ultimate questions catch up and include other types of questions such as: How do I treat others? What work am I pursuing? What kind of family am I helping to nurture? Whom do I include and support in my circle of friends and whom do I exclude? Where do I live? Who are my friends? How do I deal with difficulties, illnesses, setbacks?

In *Making Faith-Sense,* Robert Kinast spells out the process of doing theology: (1) identify an experience; (2) pay attention to feelings, thoughts and conversations; (3) consult the Scriptures, tradition, doctrine, morality; (4) ask how our experience and the tradition relate to each other; (5) decide anew how to live as Christians in the world. For example, how do our marriages or our conduct at work reflect the way Jesus Christ related to others? What image of God is operative in the ways I pass on the tradition to my children? These are *theological* questions that arise out of, and inform, the way we live out our spiritualities. Distinguishing between spirituality and theology helps us identify the different strains of our faith life. Spirituality and theology are partners that together assist us to live fully as Christians. Either one taken alone leads to a dead end. Spirituality keeps theology flexible and closely related to real life; theology helps us build our spiritual lives on a sure foundation.

We may be doing theology without realizing it. As I write, I am doing theology. As you reflect, walk, drive, ponder, question the meaning of your life as a Christian, you are doing theology. Theology searches for language and imagery to express what has been experienced in prayer. It is important for theology to be grounded in the truth of everyday living, but it goes beyond the experience itself by bringing order and meaning to our life experiences. This happens when we notice the intersection between our lives, the lives of those around us, and the life of God. Most of the time, we are content to walk along the surface of things. But as we become theologically attuned, we notice that this approach is less and less satisfying. We allow ourselves to be drawn to the rim of the events in our lives, to notice the larger contours, the mysterious depths that lie beneath them.

I have been drawn to Anglican theologian Mark McIntosh's discussion of theology.[2] For him, theology involves asking about the ultimate meaning of "real" life as it exists within the life of God. Theology involves seeing our lives as woven together with the life of God and then reflecting on the implications of this tapestry. Thus, theology is a sharing in the mystery of God's life. It is what happens when the Holy Spirit works within us bringing about the mystery of God's Word made flesh.

McIntosh relates doing theology to an experience very like one I have had. He describes gazing into the Grand Canyon for the first time and noting how unbelievably vast and beautiful it was. When I first walked to the edge of the canyon rim recently, tears of awe and gratitude rolled unexpectedly from my eyes. I was face to face with something unfathomably beautiful, huge and captivating. My body spontaneously expressed the truth that my mind would only later engage. When encountering overwhelming beauty or the magnificent power of nature, others report the urge to fall to their knees, both literally and metaphorically. McIntosh capitalizes on this experience to describe what theology is—"walking up to the edge and noticing the mystery before you." Theology "is all about sidling up to these mysteries of faith and peering into their depths."

German Jesuit Karl Rahner calls this depth dimension of life, grace. It is the presence of God that lies within every experience, every moment, every atom of creation. To be a theologian is to pay attention to the presence of God that runs like a stream through all of creation and history. Sometimes we notice because of tragedy: illness, loss of life, a failed marriage. Sometimes we notice because of beauty—large as in the Grand Canyon, or small as in the intricate design on a butterfly wing. We may notice because of a poem, a film, an idea, a conversation with a friend. Theology is about attending to mystery, the truth that beckons and speaks to us from within the fabric of existence. Theology, says McIntosh, is not separate from our everyday lives; "[I]t is the real meaning of our lives, the secret truth of them.... [T]heology is about seeking out and listening to that meaning, hearing it not just as any kind of meaning but as *God's* meaning. When we ask about meaning, theology is the tool we want to use."[3]

FOOD FOR THOUGHT

1. Describe what you understand by the term "spirituality." What does "spirituality" look like in your everyday life? Be as concrete and specific as possible. Are there theological aspects to your description?

2. Identify an issue in your life, or a social or political concern that is important to you. What bible passage comes to mind when you think and pray about this situation? How is God speaking to you through this issue? What does your reflection reveal about the nature and identity of God? Are you aware that as you go through this exercise, you are "doing theology"?

3. What do you see as the most pressing needs of the church and the world that laywomen theologians can address and to which they might bring insight and healing?

CHAPTER TWO

• SACRAMENTAL CONSCIOUSNESS •

Catholics live in an enchanted world, a world of statues and holy water, stained glass and votive candles, saints and religious medals, rosary beads and holy pictures. But these Catholic paraphernalia are mere hints of a deeper and more pervasive religious sensibility which includes Catholics who see the Holy lurking in creation. As Catholics, we find our houses and our world haunted by a sense that the objects, events, and persons of daily life are revelations of grace.[4]

This assessment of the "Catholic thing" by Andrew Greeley plunges me back into my childhood in the 1950s. The only time I acquire holy cards now is at funerals, but whether God comes close through statues, medals and holy pictures—or in nature and the evening news, Catholics have inherited a way of faith that affirms the grandeur of God "lurking" in the world. We do not need to turn away from music, dance, nature, aromas or art to reach God, for the divine is located *within* the very mysteriousness of the material world. In this chapter I discuss elements of a theology that grounds such a sacramental view of the world.

Key identifying characteristics of Roman Catholics in the 1950s— the nine first Fridays, novenas, the rosary, Friday meatless dinners— have faded. Responses to the changes vary—relief and rejoicing; a sense of loss and yearning for what seemed like a simpler time; a desire to search for new markers of Catholic identity; curiosity about these practices among the young. But the saying, "You can't go home again" applies to Catholic spirituality. If it isn't vigil lights and incense, what is it in our twenty-first-century world and church that nurtures and inspires us? How are we to renew and deepen the Catholic awareness that the sacred is tucked into every nook and cranny of reality? We cannot pass on to our children what we do not have ourselves.

When we slow down for a moment and think about our allotted span on this earth, most of us discover a desire to weave together into a seamless cloth contemplative and active modes of living—prayer and good works. This is our vocation as Christian women. But in our manic, consumer-crazed and media-saturated culture, this is no small order. Sacramental consciousness refers to a way of perceiving the world that challenges the sacred-secular dichotomy and provides a lens through which we find God in all things, great and small. Contemplation is the ability to look at the world with a long, loving gaze, and theology is well served by a contemplation that is aware of itself and intentional. This means viewing the world as God views it, with love, patience and compassion and then acting to help realize the kingdom of God.

One of my favorite poems is Adam Zagajewski's "Try to Praise the Mutilated World." Zagajewski is a Polish poet who writes in the shadow of World War II's violence and destruction. His words dwell lovingly on the simple things in life—June's long days, wild strawberries, drops of wine, the dew. He is also keenly aware that life is fragile. Ships are launched; some reach their destination; others end in "salty oblivion." His poem moves from the pain of refugees and executioners to the simple beauties of a remembered moment shared in a white room where curtains fluttered. His advice progresses from: "*try* to praise the mutilated world" to "You *must* praise the mutilated world" to "You *should* praise the mutilated world." He ends his poem: "*Praise* the mutilated world / and the gray feather a thrush lost, / and the gentle light that strays and vanishes and returns." He leads us to sacramental consciousness by noticing, describing and respecting all of reality from its ugliest tragedy to its simplest pleasure.

The Sacrament of the World and the Seven Sacraments

God is lovingly present not only in the details of the worldly theater Zagajewski describes but also in the entire cosmos—from the most magnificent galaxies to the minutest subatomic particle. There is a bond between the presence of the divine in creation and the seven sacraments of the church. Formal sacraments were instituted over time to invoke God's gracious blessing on key moments in human life. But the deepest meaning of these official sacraments is grounded in a much larger story—what we might call the liturgy of the cosmos.

Baptism: Welcomes an individual into the community of faith through symbols of cleansing water and healing oil, marked on our bodies in the form of the cross. Our faith identity is grounded in our membership in the human and cosmic community.

Eucharist: Modeled on the Jewish Seder meal that Jesus celebrated with his disciples before he died, this sacrament brings us into the presence of Jesus through the symbols of bread and wine that become Jesus' body and blood. Every meal we eat has the potential to participate in Jesus' love. Our daily meals engage us in relationships of love and call us to pray and work to alleviate the world's material and spiritual hungers.

Confirmation: An invocation of the Holy Spirit to strengthen us as adults in the faith and in our efforts to live lives of courage and love. This is the sacrament through which we "grow up" and take responsibility for ourselves and our world.

Reonciliation: An opportunity to become aware of our failure to love and to allow the Spirit to make all things new in our lives. We sin against each other and nature. Realizing our sinfulness is simply realizing the truth—a truth upon which we can build a new tomorrow in freedom and love.

Marriage: A public witness to the commitment of two persons to love and cherish each other for the rest of their lives. Marriage brings to mind the *Song of Songs* from the Hebrew Bible—a story of love between two persons. Marriage points to the many profound, intimate and passionate connections we have with others and with the world.

Holy Orders: A public witness to consecration in service to the church. This anointing and laying on of hands reminds us of baptism—the inclusive call to become servants to one another and to the world. Ordained ministry reminds us of the universal priesthood of all the faithful.

Anointing: A blessing and anointing with oil, celebrated during times of illness or nearness to death. This sacrament reminds us to pray and work for healing for the entire world. It also helps us live in gratefulness by celebrating the lives of those we know and love who are ill or near death.

When they are functioning correctly, these seven sacraments emerge out of, and lead us back to, greater awe, reverence and thanksgiving for God's grace-filled presence in the cosmos. Sacraments lead us to fall to our knees before the beauty and creativity of existence. They also provide a space to lament, rend our garments, weep and gnash our teeth at the monstrous egoism and hate all around us and in our own hearts.

The Eucharist and Daily Meals

We can concretize the relationship between a ritual sacrament and the sacrament of the cosmos by pointing to two different kinds of meals. The first is the meal we consume at Sunday Eucharist—the ritual reenactment of the story of Christ's living, dying and rising. The second involves the meals we consume every day. One is not ordinary at all; the other is quite ordinary. Some see the first as sacred and the second as secular. But can this be the case if all reality is sacred? Viewed through a sacramental lens, everyday meals can be a source of divine grace that is formalized at Sunday Eucharist. Meals of both types are times of "holy communion" during which we are present to each other, communicate, break bread and give thanks. If we believe that God is present in all aspects of our lives, it becomes possible to see dinner as a genuine

Eucharist, a place to give thanks for our participation in God's mystery-filled life.

But, you will say, what about dinners at which teenagers are squabbling, parents are arguing, babies are crying and toddlers are spilling milk and throwing spaghetti on the floor? What about dinners when there is not enough food, or too much wine or not enough time? The simple answer is that even these less-than-ideal meals can become Eucharist when we learn to view reality with a long, loving gaze. These ordinary dinners are, in fact, moments in the primordial Eucharist of the cosmos in which God gives Godself in generous and loving ways. What goes on in these everyday moments feeds and gives meaning to the ritual we share on Sunday when we come together to hear the stories, and celebrate or lament how well or poorly we have embodied the gospel during that week. In turn, Eucharist leads us back to our dinners with new sight and renewed commitment to follow in the ways of Christ. These two sacramental moments are deeply, intimately connected. Each brings God's grace to our existence in its own distinctively important ways.

Women have a long and complex history with food. Women have always been deeply engaged in its many phases: as growers, harvesters, transporters, purchasers, planners, preparers, servers and clean-up crews. Unfortunately, women are generally excluded from being waiters in very upscale restaurants, managers of food store chains and chefs. Happily, these exclusions cannot cut us off from the benefits of reflecting prayerfully on the complexities of the relationship between food and our spiritual lives. Preparing and serving food is a major way to reflect God's love, give life, nurture human bodies and help support community life. We are invited to transform our consciousness about how daily meals can become a daily participation in Eucharist, a moment in which we invite each other to thanksgiving and service.

We should aim not only to attend or participate in Eucharist, but to *become* Eucharist. This means that our lives are also marked by sadness that many of the world's poor suffer from malnutrition and famine (again the majority are women and children). Because life without adequate nourishment is dehumanizing, we remember with tears and sorrow our sisters and brothers who are without food. When we break bread together, we renew our efforts to work, lobby, donate and speak on behalf of those who are hungry. Remembrance of those without food can also enhance awareness of how we misuse food through waste, overconsumption or dieting. If we are honest, we admit that we too suffer from hunger in one way or another. We may not be without physical nourishment, but we may lack in other areas—loving well, appreciating beauty, being filled with the Spirit.

There is also a dark side to women's long connection with food. Food can provide a means of harmful control and manipulation in the interest of ego-needs gone askew. We lament the scourge of anorexia and bulimia on so many women, and have you ever sat around a table and listened to stories of family members or friends who had to validate their mother's love by consuming multiples helpings *of everything* at Sunday or holiday dinners? How are we to discern what is really going on? What motives lay behind preparing and serving food? Is this service free? Loving? The grateful love of the Eucharist helps us keep watch on our everyday Eucharists at our dining room tables with family, friends, or with the needy at a soup kitchen. I have read many wonderful prayers composed by Jewish women—this one is said as the Sabbath loaf (challah) is placed in the oven:

> Lord of all the world, in your hand is all blessing. I come now to revere your holiness, and I pray you to bestow your blessing on the baked goods. Send an angel to guard the baking...over which one recites the holy blessing—as you blessed the dough of Sarah and Rebecca our mothers. My Lord God, listen to my voice; you are the God who hears the voices of those who call to you with the whole heart. May you be praised to eternity. [5]

All of us who have meal preparation as part of our daily fare can do the same. In the many hours spent at this task, we can create a moment to say a prayer, light a candle, pour a glass of wine and practice the presence of God.

FOOD FOR THOUGHT

1. Reflect on your encounters with food this week. What were your feelings, attitudes? Motives? Where do you notice God's presence, absence in this aspect of your life? What links would you like to make between meal preparation, service, consumption and Eucharist?

2. Sift through your memories and identify an event in your everyday life in which God drew near. Share this with friends. Why do you consider this event to be "holy"?

3. As you reflect on the past week, where, when, how was the "holy" present? Devise one practice that might help you to "find God in all things" and implement it faithfully for one week. Then assess any changes in your awareness of the holy in your everyday life.

4. If the world is sacred and loved by God, how do you account for all the evil in our hearts and in conflicts throughout the world?

RITUAL

- *Become quiet.* Create a sacred space by lighting a candle and sitting in silence for a few minutes. Draw your forces together in an act of centering—become attuned to your inner rhythms, breathe slowly, deeply, evenly and begin to relax. As thoughts and worries come to mind, hold them lightly in the palm of your hand and ask God to lift them gently like a feather.

- *Music.* Play a favorite music selection—perhaps a classical piece from Mozart or Chopin, a folk song, rhythm and blues or a tune whose lyrics are especially meaningful to you. The companion CD to this series, *Called to Holiness,* offers many suitable selections. Invite the Spirit of God to suffuse the music, your space, your very being. Use the time, the silence, the music to enter directly and deeply into the people and events you encounter in your everyday life. Discover the ways in which each person and event is suffused with God's love and presence. Try to place your trust and confidence in God's providence, in God's promise to be with us in all things till the end of our days.

- *Reflect.* Focus your attention on a specific aspect of reality from the past week. You might choose something in nature; a person you have encountered; a kind act; an argument; a frustration; an illness; a meal; a daily chore. Hold this small piece of reality in your imagination and relax, quietly inviting God to shed light on how this person, event, suffering, or even sin, contains a spark of the divine. Listen to the voice of God; ask God to enlighten your mind, and open your heart to the sacraments of your daily life.

- *Find a symbol.* If possible, find (or imagine) a concrete object that symbolizes the experience, the person, the frustration, the anger, sadness or joy on which you are meditating. Touch it, get in touch with its sacredness—not only as it relates to you, but in and of itself: a stone, a blade of grass, a spoon, a book, a newspaper, a baby's rattle, a chair, a window.

- *Pray.* Take a moment to jot down your prayer, thoughts or insights. In light of this exercise identify what you desire for your life and express a brief prayer of petition, asking God for the grace that at this moment resonates at the deepest core of your being.

- *Close.* Slowly say the Our Father or a prayer of your own making.

PART TWO

• THE MANY FACES OF GOD •

Spiritual directors often ask: "What is your image of God?" It can be quite disconcerting to rattle off a description of God, only to discover that the "real" God hidden in our prayer and actions is someone altogether different. Our awareness of God has both conscious and unconscious elements, and it is possible that the God we hold in our heads is quite different from the God who operates deep in our psyches. We say that God is compassionate and loving, but when things go wrong, we may act as though God is distant and unconcerned about our suffering. Part of the theological task is to move hidden elements into awareness so that we can appreciate them, shape them, change them when necessary. When we take time to identify how we think about God's identity, we can be sure that we are engaged in the process of "doing theology."

Theologians remind us that "the image of God functions." When a religious community imagines God in exclusively male terms, it is difficult not to devalue women in the process. When the attributes of men and of God are set up as mirror images of each other, it is easy to lose sight of the metaphoric nature of language about God. Religious cultures generally assign to God those qualities that are most revered in the community. Thus, God becomes an all-powerful, all-knowing, male God. The naming of God influences our identities, the ways we do and do not value ourselves, our outlook on the world and how we relate to others. When God is seen in exclusively male terms, we conclude (wrongly) that men must be more like God than women. In turn, this perspective affects how we engage the spiritual life. As theologians, we are aware of the importance of language and imagery about God and keep tabs on how this language affects various groups within the community of faith.

Our personal images of God also deeply affect the way we live our spiritual lives. For example, a powerful, demanding, punishing God can cut off the graced-filled streams of the spiritual life altogether. A warm, fuzzy God can lead to a comfortable life without challenge or risk. Individual images of God are malleable—even though changes can temporarily upset our spiritual balance. For example, many women who abandoned an elderly, white-haired, bearded image of God experienced desolation at the loss of their long-held, familiar sense of God. With time and effort, other, more grace-filled images emerged. Artists and poets help us imagine God in fresh ways. Given the infinite nature of God, the proliferation of diverse language and imagery for God is to be preferred. The point is not to ban existing images of God in favor of new ones, but to broaden the ways we think about God in light of new developments and needs. This preference for pluralism was voiced by Thomas Aquinas who wisely commented that the whole universe together participates in the divine goodness more perfectly, and represents it better than any single creature could.

An exclusive focus on only one person of the Trinity—Father/Mother, Christ or the Holy Spirit—obscures the complex unity of the Trinity and can thwart our attempts to transform our rampant individualism into genuine sisterhood and brotherhood. It is this communitarian aspect of Trinity that we explore next.

CHAPTER THREE

• A COMMUNITY OF LOVE: TRINITY •

In those days Mary set out and went with haste to a Judean town in the hill country, where she entered the house of Zechariah and greeted Elizabeth. When Elizabeth heard Mary's greeting, the child leapt in her womb. And Elizabeth was filled with the Holy Spirit and exclaimed with a loud cry, "Blessed are you among women, and blessed is the fruit of your womb. And why has this happened to me, that the mother of my Lord comes to me? For as soon as I heard the sound of your greeting, the child in my womb leapt for joy. And blessed is she who believed that there would be a fulfillment of what was spoken to her by the Lord. (Luke 1:39–45)

This story of Mary and Elizabeth has always been special to me. I find myself collecting images of paintings of this famous meeting, many of which are very moving. In my study of medieval Christian women, I am regularly dismayed by the lack of attention to women's relationships with other women. Until recently, history has rarely deemed women's relationships with other women worthy of note. For the most part, women were seen as important because of their relationships with men. What a boon it would be if we had libraries full of stories of women's relationships with each other. Clare of Assisi's relationship with Francis is embedded in our collective memory—and not always accurately. But who knows much about Clare's relationship with Agnes of Prague? Many are aware of Catherine of Siena's relationship with Raymond of Capua, her confessor, disciple and dear friend, but much less about her relationship with her mother, her sisters or her female followers.

Happily, recent theology (especially that done by women) high-lights the importance of relationships in the Christian life—including the relationships of the persons in the Trinity. God is no longer imagined primarily as a single, lone figure, but rather as a community of love. The ultimate goal of doctrines such as that of the Trinity is to foster our relationship with God. They are intended to help Christians establish a way of perceiving and relating to the world. Ideally, doctrine expresses the community's insights into the meaning of God's presence in the world throughout time. We may or may not be conscious of the ways Trinitarian doctrine influences how we look at the world, think and behave.

Medieval texts and images show an acute awareness of the Trinity. In contrast, the doctrine of the Trinity in the twentieth century was given less prominence due to a deep preoccupation with the person of Christ. For obvious reasons, it is easier for human beings to picture and identify with the incarnate Jesus. His disciples met and walked with him, and later, members of the community wrote down the stories of his teachings and encounters with others. Less tangible are the first and third persons of the Trinity—in spite of images of the first person as an elderly male figure with flowing white hair and a beard. And then there is the ubiquitous dove, a common rendering of the Spirit.

These different doctrinal emphases should not be seen as competing with each other. Rather, we strive to make connections among them—Trinity, Creation, Incarnation and Holy Spirit. Each of these theological strains grounds and gives shape to the way we live. The tradition has often linked each of the three divine persons with specific work in the world: The Father is primary in executing the work of creation; the Son in the work of redemption; the Holy Spirit in the work of sanctification. But we are not to conclude from this division of responsibility that any person of the Trinity acts in isolation from the others. Theologians reflect on two aspects of God: first, the identity of God as Godself and the relations of the persons to each other within

the Trinity (immanent Trinity); second, the identity of God in relationship to the world (economic Trinity). We hold these two aspects of God
in creative interaction. In the chapters to follow I treat the persons of
the Trinity under the headings of creation (First Person), incarnation
(Second Person) and holiness (Third Person).

Thinking about God as a mutually present community of persons
provokes us to think about our human relationships. God speaks to
humanity through our experience, and then we devise language and
imagery to express this revelation. This is what we mean when we say
we are doing theology. Julian of Norwich, a fourteenth-century
anchoress (a religious lifestyle similar to that of a hermit) in England
had an encounter with God in the form of sixteen visions of the cross.
She reflected on it for decades (doing theology) and then recorded it in
a book called *Showings*. For Julian each person of the Trinity shares
intimately in all of the Trinity's activities. She may link the Father with
creation, the Son with redemption and the Holy Spirit with sanctification, but all three persons not only share in each act of generosity, passionate love, encouragement and protection, but they also delight in it.
We get the sense that God's greatest pleasure is loving and giving us
gifts *together, as a community of love.*

In turn, our language and imagery about God function to help us
participate in God's life, in part by creating our own communities of
love. This communal love might mean going the extra mile with someone in our families. It might involve knowing what is happening in the
lives of my neighbors and helping out when they are in need. It may
mean enjoying a Little League game with other parents, mentoring a
new colleague at work or joining a political action committee. I want to
link this image of God as a divine community of love particularly with
our experience of women's relationships with other women.

The books in this series on women reflect this renewed theological
interest in God as community of love. This theme is explored especially
in the volumes on prayer and on Latina spirituality, the latter focusing

on community and communion. Feminist theology works to bring about that aspect of the kingdom that includes equality, mutuality and love for women, as well as for all oppressed peoples. Fresh insights about the Trinity have served to ground this understanding of humanity in terms of communion. The divine community of love serves as a model for the kind of equality, mutuality and loving interaction sought in distinctive ways by women.

I have come to a deeper appreciation of the Triune God through the medieval mystics. In addition to Julian of Norwich, authors such as Hildegard of Bingen, Clare of Assisi and Catherine of Siena wrote about community and their encounters with a God who was revealed as a committed, joyous community of love and generosity. Their words convey a felt sense of this divine community of love that is attractive, alluring and beautiful. These mystics invite us to imagine a divine love feast to which we are invited. As a witness to genuine community, this image of the Trinity points us to the human potential to live our lives in loving relationship with others.

FOOD FOR THOUGHT

1. Discuss ways in which your image of God does or does not include God as Trinity. What makes the Trinity difficult or remote for you?
2. Draw a picture (in words or images) of what you consider to be an ideal community. Are you a part of such a community? Connect your ideas about loving community to the Trinity. What do you discover? In what way does your image of God affect your interactions in the various communities of which you are a part?
3. Read and discuss the story of Mary and Elizabeth as a paradigm of sisterhood reflecting the Trinity.

CHAPTER FOUR

• WE LIVE ON HOLY GROUND: CREATION •

The earth brought forth vegetation: plants yielding seed of every kind, and trees of every kind bearing fruit with the seed in it. And God saw that it was good.... God set them in the dome of the sky to give light upon the earth, to rule over the day and over the night, and to separate the light from the darkness. And God saw that it was good.... God made the wild animals of the earth...and the cattle...and everything that creeps upon the ground of every kind. And God saw that it was good.... Then God said, "Let us make humankind in our image, according to our likeness.... And it was so. God saw everything that he had made, and indeed, it was very good. (Genesis 1:12, 17–18, 25–26, 30–31)

The ecological and space movements have revolutionized our consciousness about the cosmos and the earth's place within it. Our medieval ancestors would gaze in disbelief were they to view an image that is very familiar to us—planet Earth from space. We have available to us a perspective on the cosmos that is not only awesome in its expanse, but is also truer than that of our ancestors in the faith. On the one hand, we believe that God has made us little less than the angels (see Psalm 8:5). On the other, we are an infinitesimally small speck in the larger scheme of the universe. Galaxies contain billions of stars, the largest main-sequence stars being about one hundred times the mass of the sun. The mass of supermassive black holes is between several hundreds of thousands and several million times that of our sun. Our own galaxy, the

Milky Way, consists of about two hundred billion stars, with the sun being a fairly typical specimen. It is mind-boggling to get our minds around such immensity. How small it makes us feel!

Growing awareness of our endangered ecosystems has contributed to concern for the earth. Advocacy groups across the globe work tirelessly to raise consciousness and change behaviors to reduce pollution of water, air and gases that contribute to global warming. Attending to creation should lead to enhanced care for its well-being—any and all practices, from recycling to avoiding harmful pesticides, can become elements of our spirituality.

It is unfortunate when this awareness of the vastness of creation becomes routine or mundane. Contemplating photographs of the world, other planets, galaxies or gases in space generate a sense of awe at the mystery and beauty of nature. The stories of creation in Genesis 1 and 2 belong in the ranks of the world's greatest literature. I regularly recommend to undergraduate students that when they are parents, they include the story of creation when they read bedtime stories to their children. Hearing over and over again that the world is good is a message children cannot hear too often. The Bible functions. Its stories or "myths" tell us something profound about God's identity. They reveal a God who is free; whose love extends to others; a God who is creative and generous; a God whose goodness is revealed in the beauties and complexities of nature.

It is both understandable and appropriate that our culture be engaged in debates about the relationship between the stories of science and the stories of religion. It is not our goal here to rehearse these arguments. But each of us needs to learn enough about both sets of stories so that we can harmonize belief in God with the fruits of scientific knowledge. Because science is a major element of the context in which we do theology, theology must take account of its findings. We assess our scientific worldview in the light of our belief in a loving Creator. It is possible to be a rocket scientist *and* a believer, to engage in the highest levels of research *and* to stand or kneel in awe at the beauty of nature as a reflection of Deity in both its immensity and in the minutest detail of a quark, an ant or a vein on a leaf.

The natural world is but one aspect of God's creation. Creation is extended from nature to culture when human beings, made in the image and likeness of God, use their gifts of intellect and love to create a meal, machinery, music, art, technology, spaceships to the moon. Living a contemplative existence requires fresh attention to all these phenomena. Sacramental consciousness involves allowing the world and everything and everyone in it to remind us of God by its very existence, by its very ability to "be itself." Poets are among the expert contemplatives who help us develop skills of "attending to reality." Sister M. Madeleva pays attention to the season of fall:

> Now they have come, these afternoons in November,
> When all the air is still and branches are bare,
> And the long, lovely light that I remember
> Invades with luminous peace the untroubled air. [6]

Authentic attention can lead not only to awe and praise but to weeping and action. Viewing reports of wandering refugees on the evening news with an attentive, compassionate heart leads us to identify with this suffering, to tears that humans can be so inhumane to each other and eventually to action on their behalf. Loving attention leads us into relationship with the world, to a sense of sorrow for sin and suffering and a desire to make it better. Contemplative attention can produce an awe and love of creation that generates creativity and courage to engage in gestures of help, acts of justice and prophetic words. Mary Oliver's poem about life captures the spirit of contemplative attentiveness to creation, expressing the thought that, at the end of life's journey, it would be a tragedy to have been merely a visitor in the world.

Attention to the world also leads to theology. Christian belief and trust in a God who refuses to remain in a self-contained state, hoarding divinity, is foundational to a spirituality of everyday life. Engagement with this Creator God works against complacency, spiritual blindness, boredom and indifference, and helps us nurture a sense of awe and gratitude that are at the heart of a contemplative existence. The Genesis refrain, "It was good…it was good…it was good" has the potential to open our eyes to the wonders of existence and to put us in touch with the love, generosity and creativity of God. It also provokes questions important for the present. What am I doing to help reduce harmful greenhouse gases—what kind of car do I drive? What am I doing to recycle? Do I look for products that are safe for the environment? Do I let water run with abandon when I brush my teeth or work at the kitchen sink?

We reflect on those moments in our lives that put us in touch with the beauty and suffering of creation in the light of the Bible and Tradition. Each of us has particular gifts and proclivities that lead us to concentrate on specific, concrete aspects of creation's beauty and to open ourselves to compassion and compunction for a suffering world. The world is "charged with the grandeur of God," and it also groans under the weight of war, poverty, hate, violence, genocide, starvation, illiteracy and unfreedom. A theology of creation holds us to account for both the glories and the evils of the natural and cultural worlds. It invites us to pay attention, to offer the world a long, loving gaze because it is the fruit of God's generous love. Out of such a gaze, we may be moved to extend God's action, to care for the world and its people; stand up for them whether they are leaders or lizards; behave with respect; and treat all of creation with the dignity it possesses as the work of God.

FOOD FOR THOUGHT

1. Spend ten to fifteen minutes reflecting on some aspect of nature to which you are drawn—something beautiful, or frightening and destructive. What does this meditation tell you about God? About humanity? About yourself?

2. What happens when you think of the world as God's body?

3. What does nature teach you about human life? Trees stand tall and strong, yet bend in the wind. Wind knocks out power lines and destroys homes, but also spreads seeds, clears the air and moves storm systems out to sea.

RITUALS

- As an individual, in a group, with family or in a religious education setting, do a dramatic reading of the seven days of creation (Genesis 1:1–31). Read the text slowly and meditatively. Have everyone repeat together the refrain, "And it was good." Have each person express thanks for some aspect of nature (such as the wildflowers growing along the highway) and continue to have everyone recite together after each prayer, "And it was good." Reflect on how this exercise affects your image of the first person of the Trinity.

- Design a creation calendar on which you or your family or group note for each day something good about God's creation. Use the calendar to help you celebrate New Year's Day—gratitude for the old year and welcome to the new.

- Stand still in one place and try to sense the spirit of the land. Imagine its history. Ponder its ecosystems. How do you sense the spirit of this place—sad, energetic, hopeful?

CHAPTER FIVE

• GOD BECOMES ONE OF US: INCARNATION •

Or do you not know that your body is a temple of the Holy Spirit within you, which you have from God, and that you are not your own? For you were bought with a price; therefore glorify God in your body. (1 Corinthians 6:19–20)

In his First Letter to the Corinthians, Paul wants to ensure that the members of the community view their bodily existence as dignified and good in God's sight. He wants them to know that because of Christ, bodily life has become important in a new way. The spiritual life for Christians cannot be characterized by a flight from material reality, culture or our embodied selves. Paul wanted to correct problematic behaviors in the Corinthian community—possibly incest and prostitution—but his words can legitimately help us view all aspects of bodily existence as godly. In the twentieth century, developments in both psychology and physics have led us to view the human person, indeed the entire cosmos, as unified fields. Matter is shot through with energy which is related in complex ways to space and time. Our bodies, spirits, psyches and minds are caught up in an ongoing mutually interactive dance. Christians add to this worldview a faith that Jesus' Incarnation makes the world new, shot through with divinity.

Two thousand years later Vatican II echoes Paul's conviction. "The joys and the hopes, the grief and anguish of the people of our time, especially of those who are poor or afflicted, are the joys and hopes, the grief and anguish of the followers of Christ as well. Nothing that is genuinely human fails to find an echo in their hearts."[7] What we discussed about the work of creation is advanced and deepened through the Incarnation, the Word of God become flesh.

Of the three persons of the Trinity, Christ has likely received the most ink. Traditionally, the church has put Christ at the very center of its theology and spirituality. As a fellow traveler who shared our human condition, Christ is accessible, providing a concrete flesh and blood model that inspires us to live our lives in his footsteps *(imitatio Christi)*. All of us are implicated in the Incarnation—the divine became human so that the human might become divine. It is difficult even to begin to appreciate this truth that is worth a lifetime of prayerful pondering. For Christians, the very idea of what it means to be a human being has been transformed in Jesus Christ's assumption of human form.

In the early centuries of the church, Christians discussed whether and how Jesus was divine. Many of us may still remember from early religious instruction the teaching that Jesus is one person with two natures, fully divine and fully human (as articulated at the Council of Chalcedon in 451). Depending on the needs and convictions of the faith community during various periods of the church's history, believers emphasized either the divine Christ (Christology from above) or the human Jesus (Christology from below). The Infant of Prague reflects the former—an image of a small but regal Christ, dressed as a king and standing on Mary's lap. The message of this image is that Jesus is a royal, powerful person, holding a scepter or a globe of the world. In dramatic contrast are images of a very human Jesus, the rosy-cheeked baby playing at Mary's feet, or the comforter, the man of sorrows, suffering and bleeding on the cross.

Language about Christ changes as well. In the last fifty years, theologians have moved away from more abstract, philosophical language, in favor of stories of Jesus' life, ministry, death and resurrection. It is worthwhile to take a few minutes each week outside of Sunday liturgy to read a story about Jesus. In prayer, we inquire about who this Jesus

was and allow his life to touch us by reflecting on how the story rever-
berates with our experience. When you read these stories with fresh
eyes, they are amazing indeed. Our biblical, theological and historical
knowledge of Jesus Christ is connected to our risking a personal relationship with him. Theology enriches our ideas *about* Jesus Christ and
then leads beyond to a relationship in which we accept and love him as
a divine-human person. African American spirituals such as "I Want
Jesus to Walk with Me" suggest what such a genuine, human relationship with Christ might be like.

At any given time, depending on the circumstances and the
rhythms of life, we are drawn to one or another specific aspect of
Christ. A friend who enjoys a glass of wine each evening jokingly
reminds us that turning water into wine was Jesus' first miracle! (see
John 2:1–11). Perhaps you find special meaning in the story of Mary
Magdalene's relationship with Jesus (Luke 8:2; Luke 23:55; John
20:1–2, 17); or the feeding of the five thousand (Luke 9:10–17); or
Jesus' gestures to the woman at the well (John 4:1–42); the woman with
the issue of blood (Mark 5:25–34); or the woman about to be stoned
for adultery (John 8:1–11); the Jesus of Gethsemane (Matthew
26:36–56) or Emmaus (Luke 24:13–35). It can be challenging to find
meaning in stories we may have heard since childhood, but taking a
moment to pay attention to them in light of pressing issues in our lives
is a great spiritual practice. We discover things about ourselves and our
relationship with God as we read, watch for movements in our hearts,
pause and pray.

That Christianity is a historical religion professing a God who is
deeply engaged in the affairs of the world makes a difference in the way
we look at the world and live. In assuming human flesh, Christ adds yet
another level of holiness to the world—the natural world, the bodies
and spirits of humans, the planets, the entire universe. We even believe
that good can come out of the evils of human sin and suffering. This
embodied nature of Christianity means that everything about us is

relevant to our spiritual lives—family, work, learning, playing, finances, age, sex, geography.

Such an outlook may be attractive, useful, expedient, convenient, edifying—but it is also *theological*. What we do in our bodily existence every day matters because of creation and incarnation. The point of a series on women's spirituality is neither to privilege nor cast in stone "women's experience," but it does aim to hold up, celebrate and nurture the concrete, historical, embodied nature of our spiritual lives *as women*. The history of the human race is rife with examples of negative, generalized gender stereotypes that constrict and penalize women simply for being women.

We keep watch to guard against perpetuating harmful images or understandings of women that impede the fullness of our lives with God and each other. Consider a story about a fifth-grade swim team. A donation of free, *pink* caps created a dilemma until one mom suggested that all the children—boys as well as girls—wear the pink caps at a competition to acknowledge and celebrate women. The boys as well as the girls enthusiastically worked to convince the coach to give his OK. This is a small, humorous anecdote, but it symbolizes our slow liberation from stereotyped, gendered conditioning. Beyond pink swim caps, we learn to attend carefully to the needs and desires women voice and empower women to be fully alive in the Spirit as they go about shaping their lives amidst the struggles of existence. Women's experience in all its enculturated particularity is sacred business— theologically and spiritually.

FOOD FOR THOUGHT

1. We are asked to imitate Christ and yet we live in circumstances dramatically different from his. Identify one deep, enduring aspect of Jesus' life and discuss how women might "imitate" it in the world of the twenty-first century.

2. Those of us who call ourselves Christian live with a name that includes the name of "Christ," the anointed one. As a Christian woman describe the Jesus of your spirituality. Who is the Jesus you would like to have in your spiritual life?

RITUAL

- Place your Bible on a table with a burning candle.
- Step back and reflect on its significance (or lack thereof) in your life. What does it mean to reverence this book? Would the world be any different for you if we did not have this book? How much do you know about what is inside this book compared to other books you might have in the house? What blocks you from wanting to know more about its contents?
- Choose a story from one of the four Gospels. You may have a favorite or you may simply want to open the Bible randomly and take pot luck. Read the text slowly out loud to yourself, your children or a group.
- Discuss what the story means to you. Does it relate in any way to your life or the lives of your friends and loved ones?
- Say a brief prayer of thanksgiving for the wisdom contained and blow out the candle.

CHAPTER SIX

• HOLY POWER, HOLY PRESENCE: THE HOLY SPIRIT •

Come, Creator, Spirit,
visit the souls of your own;
fill with heavenly grace
the breasts that you have created.
You who are called Paraclete,
gift of the most high God,
living water, flame, charity
and spiritual anointing;
You who are sevenfold in your gift,
finger of God's right hand,
you who were rightly promised by the Father,
enrich our throats with speech.
Inflame the light of our senses,
pour love into our hearts,
the weakness of our bodies
strengthen with lasting power.
Drive the enemy far back,
and at once grant us peace;
with you going ahead of us,
may we avoid all harm.
Through you may we know the Father
and recognize the Son;
and may we always believe
in you, Spirit of both. [8]

How much my life would change for the better if I memorized this prayer and began each day praying it! The metaphors in this hymn get our theological senses in tune. Imagining the Spirit as the finger of God's hand is a Trinitarian statement about the mutual cooperation of the Father and the Spirit. We find out about who we are as children of God in the statements about God giving us the Spirit who brings grace and charity into our lives. The Spirit is imagined as water, fire and oil— what associations do you make with these very earthy elements? This prayer allows us to pray about our deepest desires—inspired speech, alert senses, loving hearts, strong bodies, safety and peace. Finally, it attests to the belief—first articulated in John's Gospel (14:25–26; 16:13)—that the power of the Spirit enables us to know about, and live out of, God's saving love.

Theologians often lament that the Holy Spirit has been neglected in the tradition. Words like amorphous, faceless, forgotten, upstaged, vacant, unclear and invisible pop up everywhere. Theologian G.J. Sirks compares the Holy Spirit to Cinderella (the one who does all the hard, dirty work in the cellar and gets no recognition for it).[9] Kilian McDonnell has called for a renewed awareness of the Spirit through what he calls "pneumatological affirmative action."[10] But the Spirit is more present than we may think. For it is only through the Spirit that we come to know God, live our faith life with love and intelligence, and make all things new.

Most often the Spirit is imagined as a dove or as tongues of fire. In many cultures, the dove was used to symbolize a messenger from the divine realm, or the free flight of our spirits to God in death or ecstasy. The plaintive call of the mourning dove symbolized love and fertility. In other cases, the dove represented reason, virtue, purity or peace. You may remember the story of the flood in which Noah sends out a dove from the ark to see if the flood has receded (Genesis 6:1–12). In the New Testament, the dove shows up as the vehicle of Mary's impregnation at the Annunciation. Thus in a real sense, the Spirit is a source of the Incarnation (Luke 1:26–8). The dove is also the bearer of the message at Jesus' baptism that the Father was well pleased with him (Luke 3:21–22). And at Pentecost, the apostles and disciples in the Upper Room receive the Spirit in the form of wind and tongues of fire (Acts 2:1–4).

The Spirit is particularly important to laity, and in a distinctive way, to women. Vatican II gave birth to an age of the laity. It is a challenge to develop a more horizontal, inclusive way of structuring the church when it has long been accustomed to locating power at the top. Women and all other marginalized groups have a special responsibility to open themselves to the Spirit, to participate in, and contribute to, a renewed pneumatology (theology of the Holy Spirit). We extend the discrete event of confirmation throughout our entire lives by asking for gifts and fruits, and risking ourselves to use them for the common good. It is not surprising that Pentecostalism is one of the fastest growing Christian movements in the world. Christians all over the world long for and experience the power of the Spirit's work within individuals and communities.

The idea that the Spirit does have a distinct, personal face has been used to support and encourage the gifts of laity. The anonymity of the Spirit is interpreted to mean that the Spirit assumes the face of every Christian who allows the Spirit to work within her. Through the Spirit, we have the potential to be witnesses to the face of God. In addition, it is in and through the Holy Spirit that we are able to know God, that God is able to know us, and that we are able, in grace, to live and love in godly ways. The Spirit is the force through which we become extensions of the communitarian love of the Trinity.

In the New Testament, the Greek words for *energy* and *dynamism* point to the positive force for good that we possess because of grace, the work of God in the world. In most cultures, power is associated with men and carries negative connotations. Power is dangerous and corrupting and has great potential to become sinful. But it is important for women to recall that the Christian tradition associates the Holy Spirit with activities that involve good power in which we are invited to partake.

The Spirit is the power that enables reconciliation, allowing us to forgive small and even great offenses; the power that invites us to live our lives intelligently as well as lovingly; the power to serve others. The Spirit casts out the fears that bind us and prevent us from living in the freedom of the daughters and sons of God (see Romans 8:14). The Spirit guides the church as it struggles to be faithful to gospel values; the Spirit is the Comforter, the bond of love between the Father and the Son; the power that gives us the courage to name and face up to our sinfulness. Persons benefit from this Spirit power in ways dependent on their personalities, history, family and particular context.

Two operations of the Spirit are of special importance to women in the twenty-first century. The first is prophecy, the divinely inspired energy that confronts the status quo and points the community in new, more godly, directions. In the past, women called by the Spirit to confront evil and preach conversion were particularly suspect, and were often silenced or even killed because of their perceived "emotional" susceptibility to evil spirits. Stereotyping and silencing women's prophetic voices need to be roundly confronted. Women, whose rich perspectives have been obscured and rejected in the past, are called to step forward, to open themselves to the voice and courage of the Spirit. The church and the world need women's voices more than ever.

Prophets usually meet a bad end. People will not like us if we speak the truth to power. Fear of losing status, power, possessions or reputation, blocks the Spirit. We go to great lengths to preserve the illusion that things are not *really* as bad as we think. We are called by the Spirit to keep two images before us—a mutilated world torn by war, famine, torture, illness, violence and poverty (the majority of its sufferers being women and children); and the image of the apostles freed by the Spirit from fear, timidity and hiding into confident preachers of the gospel.

These images stand like beacons, beckoning us to pray for courage, discern and become voices for justice, freedom and truth.

It is hard work to discern the difference between authentic revelation that genuinely renews church and world and self-serving movements that betray the Spirit's truth. It takes guts to speak out and stand up for the good. Thus, we pray not to become faint of heart or ignore the Spirit's call for justice. The Scriptures warn us not to quench the Spirit (see 1 Thessalonians 5:19; Ephesians 4:30). We know that the stories of prophets inevitably include an initial response of fear to the Spirit's call. But we also believe that the Spirit has the power to cast out the fear that kills our spirits and stifles our work for justice.

A second important gift of the Spirit for women is the Spirit's promise to make all things new (see Revelation 21:5). For those who have spent most of history living on the "underside"—the marginal, the oppressed, the voiceless—it is imperative to hope and trust that the Spirit has the power to transform the world. This hope motivates us to roll up our sleeves and work toward new beginnings. These fresh starts may be as small as a slight attitude adjustment within our own hearts, or as large as helping to change a law or assist women who need help at crucial turning points in their lives.

Life without the power to change course is a form of hell. To be resigned to second-class citizenship for women, persons of color, the poor, the elderly, the ill is a life none of us cares to live. Imagine not being able to start over, offer or receive forgiveness, renew a broken relationship, get a new job or watch the flowers come up in the spring. The Spirit is associated with transforming hearts and minds. A woman in a spirituality group spoke about how the Spirit empowered her to overcome a "learned helplessness" she had been taught as the only female child in her family. The Spirit is the vehicle by which we leave off the old self bound by sin, slavery, fear and egoism, and embrace the new, open to grace and freedom and love (see Romans 6:6; Ephesians 4:22; Colossians 3:9).

In their diversity and particularity, women are called to collaborate with the Spirit and with each other. The Spirit demands that we place our particular gifts at the service of the specific needs and sufferings of women at this moment in history.

> [W]e also boast in our sufferings, knowing that suffering produces endurance, and endurance produces character, and character produces hope, and hope does not disappoint us, because God's love has been poured into our hearts through the Holy Spirit that has been given to us (Romans 5:3–5).

We know well that this passage from Paul about suffering can no longer be used to tell women to suffer in silence against their wills. The Christian tradition has been misused by emphasizing, even glorifying, suffering as redemptive in situations that only increased oppression. Women in abusive marriages are told to "tough it out"; slaves were told that their condition was the will of God; many grew up thinking that if it didn't hurt, life must not be worthy. Rather, this passage from Romans reminds us of the superabundance of God's love poured into our hearts and into the world through the Spirit. Indeed, we can call upon the Spirit to heal the wounds of the wrongful suffering inflicted upon women simply because they are women. As we work to right the ills of the world, we need to keep in view images of abundance— Niagara Falls, huge vats of wine poured out, a sudden summer rainstorm, the swells of the ocean—to remind ourselves of the magnificent, magnanimous pouring out of the Spirit's gifts upon us.

Many metaphors for the Spirit are related to *life*—wind, breath, water, fire, service, risk, reconciliation, love. To have and to be Spirit means to be alive in every aspect of life—personal, professional, spiritual, intellectual, cultural, sexual, ecological. Spirituality has to do with the *eros* or longing of the universe, the potential for holy power and presence beyond our finite existence. We are free to embrace and develop spirit, to detach our restlessness and anxiety from consumer instincts and reattach them to love. Ronald Rolhesier reminds us:

> Long before we do anything explicitly religious at all, we have to do something about the fire that burns within us. What we do with that fire, how we channel it, is our spirituality, whether we want one or not, whether we are religious or not.[11]

What a gift that we are free to use the words "Holy Spirit" to name our deepest hopes and joys, our comfort in suffering and failure, the push to have courage and take risks, the joy of renewal. Presupposing that we are made in God's Trinitarian image, the Spirit names what we want for ourselves—who we want to become—in our most sane, honest, loving and grace-filled moments. The Spirit provides the energy for action that has the common good of all in view, especially the poorest among us.

In the northeast corner of France, early in the eighteenth century, Jean-Pierre de Caussade, S.J., gave a series of conferences on the spiritual life for a group of nuns. At the conclusion of these lectures, de Caussade reminded the nuns that through faith, Jesus continues to live and work among us through the Holy Spirit.

> We are in an age of faith; the Holy Spirit no longer writes gospels, except in our hearts; saintly souls are the pages, suffering and action the ink. The Holy Spirit is writing a living gospel with the pen of action, which we will only be able to read on the day of glory when, fresh from the presses of life, it will be published. O what a beautiful story! What a beautiful book the Holy Spirit is now writing! It is in press; not a day passes when the type is not being set, the ink not applied, the pages not being printed.[12]

With modifications to accommodate our computer age, de Caussade's analogy for the Holy Spirit as one who writes a living gospel reaches out to us across the centuries. Consciousness of the Spirit's lively presence grows slowly and in different ways: The Spirit visits in prayer; conversations about the Spirit take place; the Spirit is recognized in compassionate action for justice; sermons are heard; books and articles are written and read. The sheer variety of encounters with the Holy Spirit quickens us to attend to the particular shape this holy power takes in our lives and world, and then to know about, and be account-able to, the long history of our ancestors' experiences of Spirit.

FOOD FOR THOUGHT

1. When you hear the word *power* what comes to mind? What positive or negative associations do you have with this term? What happens when you link the idea and practice of power with the Holy Spirit?
2. In the Christian tradition, the Holy Spirit is most often represented with a dove. Is this an adequate image for you? Identify two or three fresh images that perhaps more adequately reflect the being and role of the Holy Spirit in your life.
3. Take a moment to reflect on the major fears in your life. What hap-pens when you allow the breath of the Spirit to blow through them?

CHAPTER SEVEN

• GOD AND GENDER •

When I behold your heavens, the work of your fingers,
the moon and the stars which you have set in place—
what is humanity that you should be mindful of us?
Who are we that you should care for us?
You have made us barely less than God,
and crowned us with glory and honor.
You have made us responsible
for the works of your hands... (Psalm 8:3–6) [13]

This psalm celebrates the loving generosity of God and the ultimate beauty and dignity bestowed on the human person, female and male. The story of creation in Genesis underlines this exalted image of humanity, reminding us that everyone is made in the image and likeness of God, called to participate in the life, love and holiness of God— Father/Mother, Christ and Spirit.

Of course it is literally impossible to see ourselves through God's eyes. Nevertheless, we must use our imaginations to try. Some persons think too much of themselves, others too little. Throughout its history, the Christian tradition has based its anthropology on maleness and described women as missing the mark of the male norm of intelligence, holiness, inner beauty and God-likeness. This is a difficult legacy to overcome. But thanks to new interest and research on women's history and holiness—from the Bible to the twenty-first century—we are discovering anew creative, courageous holy women on whose shoulders we stand and whose virtues inspire us. It will take many lifetimes to right the wrongs of the past toward women. And yet the tradition also provides resources, clues, pointers and models to help us persevere in the journey toward a greater sense of the divine call to women as well as men.

We are slowly learning that we need to speak of God as neither male nor female or both male and female. Since the tradition has consistently thought about God in personal terms, gendered nouns and pronouns easily spring to our lips. But this does not preclude thinking about God as light, a rock, a rainbow. All language about God is metaphorical, not literal. Elizabeth Johnson's work *She Who Is: The Mystery of God in Feminist Theological Discourse* provides a solid foundation for thinking about God theologically from the perspective of gender. Johnson repeatedly calls us back to the truth that doctrines of God function by affecting our identities, values and behaviors. An exclusively male God has never served women well—spiritually, psychologically, socially, historically or economically. Our images and language about God affect our everyday life for good or ill, and our ways of being female and male, in turn, affect the ways in which we picture and think about God.

Gender is also a relevant category when it comes to our understanding of Christ. As noted above, the fact that God was incarnated as a male human being is a factor in our theologies of Incarnation. It is necessary to distinguish between the identity of Jesus as a Jewish male born in first-century Palestine and his role as savior of the human race. The crux of salvation is not that Jesus was male but that he was a human being. Women who need to address the relationship between Jesus' maleness and women's status in the church may posit a range of theological questions. In what sense are women made in God's image, called as equals to God's love, the fullness of holiness and as witnesses to God's presence in the world? For others, this has never been an issue. They easily locate Jesus' inclusive redemptive love in his humanity, not in his maleness. In either case, Jesus' existence as a male means that he did not go through life as a female. It is salutary to explore what this means for women, the community of faith and our various theologies. What are the distinctive ways in which women are called to be the presence and action of Christ in the world?

Because women have so often been marginalized or excluded from aspects of religious history (*misogyny*, from the Greek term for "hatred of women," refers to this exclusion), we have a pressing task to explore and experiment with ideas about God that include women and their experience. Women have always been called by God to open themselves to the divine gifts and the Spirit's power. God desires women to see themselves as persons called and embraced by the divine into the fullness of humanity and to share in the divine life. We are called to know and love God out of the distinct experiences of our lives as women which include loving our neighbor, living lives of integrity and working for justice and peace.

Many women experience a profound sense of loss when they discover that they no longer identify with images of God that use only male terminology and imagery. It requires a great deal of sweat and tears to move to more encompassing images of God that include female attributes and imagery—wisdom/Sophia, mother, nurse, aunt, grandmother, crone/wise woman. The goal of this quest for more inclusive God imagery is the realization of the Spirit's call to the heights of holiness for women. This holiness is incarnated in ways that are distinctive to women's history and experience, and empowers their particular, historical, theological dreams and hopes for the future.

Theology With Women in the View Finder

Theological reflection on the tradition in light of women's experience has resulted in a range of theologies that place the "woman question" front and center. Such feminist theologies argue that our talk about God should be directly related to the recognition, freedom and dignity of women. For some, the term *feminist* is a stumbling block, but at its best, feminist theology assists women, inviting them to be full participants in the Christian story and in life in general. Too often, women associate the term *feminist theology* with radical ideas, bra-burning and hatred of men. But if we define feminist theology as ordered, prayerful reflection on the experience of women in light of God's desire for our freedom and fullness of life, it becomes a platform from which many women of diverse backgrounds can begin a conversation about their faith.

Feminist theology includes a number of "moments" or tasks. First, it works to recover the forgotten or obscured past of our female ancestors in the faith—often called *herstory*. We are now more aware of women in the Bible and in all other periods of the church's history who struggled, as we do, to love God as disciples of Jesus Christ. Feminist theology is finding ever-new ways to interpret this material in light of our present context. Eventually, the story of Christian women will become integrated into the total story that until now has focused too exclusively on men.

Second, feminist theology raises questions about aspects of the Christian tradition that are seen as unhelpful, even harmful, to women. For example, rules that prevent the community from hearing women's voices about their experience of God seem singularly inappropriate in a culture of educated, articulate Christian women. Theologians interpret this tradition, raising questions about the status quo (a hermeneutics of suspicion) and searching for ways to bring women's experience of God to the fore (a hermeneutics of openness). A critical assessment of the tradition assists women to be more and more open to the Spirit's gifts and fruits.

A third task of feminist theology is reconstruction. Building upon a critical assessment of the tradition vis-à-vis women, theologians offer new interpretations, more inclusive ritual and creative ideas about how to think about God that include, serve and honor the experiences of Christian women. An example is the expanded roles of women in liturgy and ministry since Vatican II. Feminist theologies were first initiated by white, Western women, but quickly feminist theology expanded to include women of color. There are now *Latina* and *mujerista* (*mujer* is the Spanish word for "woman") perspectives. *Womanist* theology articulates Christianity through the lens of African American women, and Asian women are also finding their own theological voices based on their experiences in countries such as Korea *(minjung theology)* and India.

Feminist theology emphasizes practical activity. It aims not only to *think* theologically, but to *act* to transform the world. In this new world order which reflects aspects of God's kingdom, women will no longer be denied human dignity. They will be protected by the law; be free of violence, abuse and rape; receive food, housing and education; be empowered to make choices according to their values; make decisions about marriage and friendship; be able to work and raise their children in an environment conducive to health and growth.

As with theology in general, feminist theology needs to be done by both professional theologians and ordinary women across the globe. Our mandate is to love women into speech, to call forth the voices of women. In this hugely diverse world of women's experience, we ask again:

> How do we experience God?
>
> What does the term *Good News* mean in our everyday lives? What is good about it? What is news?
>
> What names do we give to God and why? Do these names point to what we need from God?
>
> What images do we have for God?
>
> What images do we think God has for us?
>
> What is our relationship with God like?
>
> What are our deepest desires for ourselves, our loved ones, the world?
>
> What brings us life and freedom in the Spirit?
>
> What brings slavery and death?

Whether we think alone or get together to discuss such questions, we are doing feminist theology. Without this grassroots knowledge, expression and conversation, there is no way for women's experience of God to be incorporated into the wider theological dialogue.

One effective vehicle for doing this kind of theology is narrative. We all have stories to tell. At times, we are simply telling stories in order to share or get to know each other. But when we tell these stories in the context of the stories of the Christian faith, we are no longer simply telling stories, but doing theology. In every story there lurks a theology and most theology can be traced to a story. But feminist theology does not stop at stories, since it is a theology committed to improving the concrete, everyday lives of women everywhere. It is hard to imagine that the lives of men would not also be improved, although women finding voice and freedom can be deeply uncomfortable and even disturbing to many men and women—which brings us back to the theme of power.

Power is the ability to get things done. It may include getting food, voting or passing new legislation, obtaining an education, taking out a mortgage, getting a line of credit or being free to express ideas. In Christian terms, the power of the Spirit involves all of these activities but with one significant addition. The context and motive is love—working toward a common good in the name of the Father/Mother, Son and Holy Spirit. The gifts of the Spirit are a godly power enabling all our earthly endeavors. The goal is to abandon manipulative power or power *over* others, in favor of power *with and for* others, power that builds up and brings life.

When certain groups have exercised power for a long time, it is difficult and often impossible for them to surrender, transform and share their power with others. But we cannot give up on this goal of including the entire community, especially women and the poorest among us, in this holy power. The ultimate model for this kind of power is the divine community of love, a love that endured even to death on a cross, and to the sending of the Spirit to dwell in every heart and empower us to help bring about the kingdom of God. In the Spirit, God offers all Christians the authority and the responsibility to name, claim and shape the faith. The eucharistic meal provides a model of church in which the door is open to everyone. The church is always called to reform, to stand judged before God and to be open to voices that have been silenced. Only in an open, inclusive community can we nurture the kind of renewed vitality in the Body of Christ that will allow it to grow, deepen and thrive in the twenty-first century.

Afterword: God Is Not…!

I cannot bring our conversation about God to a close without calling attention to a little-known aspect of the Christian tradition. After pages of words, ideas and images about God it is time to remember that God was, is, and always will be, *beyond* our words, ideas and images. The reality of God eludes all our attempts to name or imagine deity in any medium. When we focus on our inability to name God, we use terms such as *ineffable* and *transcendent*. These words point to that aspect of God that is above, beyond and outside all human efforts to name God. It may be helpful to offer an example from human life—falling in love. Have you ever tried to tell someone what it is like to fall in love? We humans make some admirable attempts. We use words, we write poetry, we sing, dance, offer random hugs or simply shout to anyone who cares to hear. But in the end, when the love is deep and long and true, we end up in silence. No words, images or music can quite capture what it is like to love and be loved.

This kind of theology is called *negative theology* (Latin: *via negativa;* Greek: *apophatic,* which means "not able to be spoken"). This type of theology is important for the entire community of faith but especially for women. Negative theology reminds us that our words, ideas and images of God can never do more than point to a God who is beyond us. To realize this truth is to know deep in our being, the smallness of our individual existence, even the smallness of the cosmos, next to God's immensity. Our response is to fall on our knees, to weep in joy, to stand silent before the Creator of the universe.

If negative theology is not alive and well, we are prone to the dangers of literalism and idolatry. In the case of literalism, we mistake the metaphor for the reality. God is not *literally* a person. God is not *literally* a rock. God is not *literally* male or female. In the case of idolatry we are fooled into thinking that the language and imagery we use for God *is* God. If we find ourselves angry and upset about calling God "Mother" it may be because we have forgotten that the word "Father" is not God, but only points to an aspect of God.

For thousands of years, the human race has found ways to name God. This type of theology is called *positive theology* (Latin: *via positiva;* Greek: *kataphatic,* or "through speech"). I think of Saint Francis of Assisi as the quintessential example of a positive theologian, since he saw God in the trees and in the birds, and even in the wolves. And yet I feel quite confident that Francis never mistook his language about God for God's very self. All we can do is point to God. We identify those qualities in our experience that we value highly and we attribute them to God. We use human experience to talk about God, but the divine and the human are not identical realities.

These two ways of naming God go hand in hand. The positive and negative ways make sense only when they remain in mutual relationship. Most of us are probably most familiar with the positive way, but we remain mindful that our words and images do not fully capture the meaning of God. Below is a schema of both ways of approaching God—both columns being true.

God is good	God is *not* good/*beyond* good in the way we know good
God is powerful	God is *not* powerful/*beyond power* in the way we know power
God is love	God is *not* love/*beyond* love in the way we know love

God is Father	God is *not* Father/beyond Father as we know Father
God is Mother	God is *not* Mother/*beyond* Mother the way we know Mother

The qualities we attribute to God are an attempt to name what cannot be named, to bring God close, to understand God in accessible ways. But God is not *literally* white or black, tall or short, fat or thin, above or within. We need as much inclusive variety as we can muster when we talk about God, but when we understand God as both male and female, and neither male nor female, we preserve God's transcendent, mysterious otherness and God's intimate closeness.

FOOD FOR THOUGHT

1. Do you consider yourself a feminist? Why or why not? How do you describe your efforts to work for the full inclusion of women in the community of faith?
2. What language do you use for God? Are there ways you would like to expand your vocabulary and imagery about God? How so?

• THEOLOGY AND THE SPIRITUAL LIFE •

Throughout this excursion into the world of grassroots theology, we have underlined the importance of keeping theology grounded in the "real life" of faith and of keeping faith informed and shaped by theology. Experience and reflection go together like ham and eggs or peanut butter and jelly. In part three, we move from explicit theological reflection on God's identity to our response to God's love. Parts one and two functioned as the theological foundation of our daily living—what we call our spirituality or, more narrowly, ethics. Our experience shapes our ideas about God, and our ideas about God influence the way we behave and live. The questions "Who Am I?" and "Who is God?" need to be in constant conversation with each other.

I have chosen two practical areas that I think have special importance for women today. The first addresses the rampant consumer culture in which we live and asks how we respond, as Christians, to the constant bombardment of media images and marketing techniques. Traditional language refers to this aspect of the spiritual life as self-sacrifice—the aspect of our spiritual lives that we associate with Lent. Practices might include fasting, sexual abstinence or solitude on the one hand; or engaging in active work for the benefit of others on the other— volunteering with Habitat for Humanity, helping in a soup kitchen or working to change unjust laws. Motivations for such practices include solidarity with the poor, the desire to make an offering to God, purification, atonement for sin, avoidance of evil or waking ourselves up as spiritual beings, in order to help others.

Virtually all religions engage in periods of "giving things up" or doing penance. The Jewish celebration of Yom Kippur is a solemn period of fasting and reflection. As a Jew, Jesus would have participated in this practice. In times of national crisis, the prophets counseled the community to fast, to repent, to alter habitual behavior in order to wake up to some present or impending disaster. Muslims fast for an entire month from sunup to sundown during the holy season of Ramadan. Ironically, in affluent, consumer-oriented countries that could benefit most from such religious practices, gestures of sacrifice seem to be diminishing rather than growing.

Our second topic is virtue. Theologians identify three theological virtues (faith, hope and love) and four cardinal virtues (prudence, justice, fortitude and temperance). Other related virtues include patience, fidelity, perseverance, humility, openness, generosity, simplicity and the like. Virtues are often juxtaposed with vices—pride works against humility; conspicuous consumption works against simplicity of life; bigotry and prejudice undermine openness. Because theology has been done almost exclusively by men, our ideas of virtue have emerged out of the ways men experience the world. For example, we need to ask whether pride from a female perspective looks the same as it does from a male perspective. Happily, we have begun to think anew about all theological topics in light of the experience of the female members of the faith community.

CHAPTER EIGHT

• "LENT COMES TO YOU": THE WAY OF ASCETICISM •

The term asceticism *has its origins in a Greek word that means "exercise" or* "training." Originally it meant physical training—as in preparing for the Olympics. Athletes practice until every muscle is tuned to top performance. Such training involves a good deal of sacrifice. It means long hours in the gym or at the track, a rigorous diet and abstaining from certain pleasures. You may recognize this experience if you are a runner, soccer player or tennis buff. Others who have mastered a musical instrument or a foreign language or spent months in physical therapy will also recognize this process. When you hear a pianist play a Bach fugue with effortless spontaneity, you know she has logged thousands of hours practicing. Through sustained, disciplined behaviors, what was halting and difficult becomes easy and full of grace. Through guidance, repetition and refinement, motions become second nature, no longer requiring painstaking attention.

As Christianity moved into the Greek world in the first century, it made use of this idea to explain the spiritual life. The idea of asceticism in the physical realm was extended to include not only physical training, but mental, spiritual and ethical development as well. Through sustained practice, we learn to cooperate with God's grace to live lives of virtue and holiness. For example, we might decide to attend to daily speech and behaviors through a simple reflection at the end of the day to assess our decisions, actions and words in light of the gospel. Gradually it becomes easier to notice the difference between harmless blowing off steam and harmful gossip. We become skilled at catching ourselves in sinful behaviors and changing course toward greater love. After weeks, months and even years of practice, being good becomes easier. We speak in love with grace and spontaneity, just like the pianist playing the Bach fugue.

The tradition has included extreme ascetic practices. Desert fathers and mothers in the fourth century and some medieval monks, nuns and laypersons engaged in harsh denial of all sensual pleasure and even inflicted physical pain on their bodies. It is difficult for most of us to understand the value of such practices, and they are not popular as tools for a contemporary asceticism. In our context, a recommendation for any type of fasting needs to consider the prevalence of eating disorders such as anorexia and bulimia. Feminist scholars, especially, are critical of past ascetic practices that connected matter/woman/body with sin and death, recommending the suppression or destruction of the physical in the interests of "higher" spiritual values. The integration of the body into our spiritual practices has opened new doors to the role of the material in the spiritual life. Many of us pray and experience God's presence when walking, running, doing yoga, hiking and mountain climbing—to name a few examples.

While some feminist theologians remain skeptical about asceticism because of its dualistic implications (body versus spirit), others have attempted to transform its meaning. Asceticism is an effective way to deconstruct harmful, socially conditioned stereotypes of self as woman or man in the interest of creating new, life-giving self-definitions, marked by love, equality and mutuality. For example, spending an hour a week at a women's shelter can shake up my ingrained image of myself; open up my understanding of other ways women exist in the world; or allow me to enter into fresh relationships that are unpretentious and life-giving.

Ascetic practices can also serve to dismantle compulsive, addictive behaviors in favor of liberation and fullness of life—both sensual and intellectual—that have been buried beneath dulling, routinized patterns of living and consuming. If you have ever engaged in an extended fast, you quickly realize how deeply structured our days are by breakfast, lunch and dinner. When these three meals are removed, we realize how focused we are on food. More time becomes available because we don't have to think about, prepare or eat meals. All of a sudden, we have some unexpected time on our hands. A friend of mine told me that she experienced a poignant mix of sorrow and new discovery after her husband died and they no longer shared three meals a day together.

Third, asceticism can be understood in relational, sociopolitical terms. Self-denial can result in enhanced sensitivity, compassion and solidarity with the poor, leading to action on their behalf. We can choose to live more simply or alter behaviors that endanger fragile ecosystems. In a more general vein, asceticism can shore up our sense of freedom, joy, courage and fullness of life. Most of us function on only one cylinder. Used in a thoughtful and creative fashion, asceticism can wake us up, energize us, tap into our creative wellsprings and open up the windows of our lives to let God and others in.

Throughout this extended conversation on women and theology, we acknowledge that speaking of women in general has a role, but not unless we remember that ultimately, there is no generic, common "woman." Each of us is unique and our experience varies broadly. Genuine asceticism will assume different forms, depending on where we live, whether we are poor or rich or middle class, at war or in peace, young, middle-aged or senior. Family circumstances and occupation are also relevant. And as important as this type of asceticism is to help us cope with our addiction-ridden, consumer-oriented culture, there is another type of asceticism that could prove even more important to our spiritual lives as twenty-first–century women.

Aceticism in a New Key

The kind of asceticism we have been discussing thus far involves a voluntary, systematic program of self-discipline. The image of a thin, gray-cloaked monk with solemn visage and sunken cheeks comes to mind.

But there is another kind of asceticism that is not at all voluntary, does not involve monasticism and affects everyone—the asceticism of everyday life. This kind of asceticism is captured by the expression "You do not need to go to Lent; Lent comes to you."

This type of asceticism conjures up a quite different image from that of a monk. We imagine rather a woman, whose days are filled with any combination of responsibilities, children, friends, work, house, garden, meals, chauffeuring, community service, illness, hot flashes, elderly parents and on and on. This type of asceticism focuses on responding creatively and in love to the demands and suffering that is integral to daily life. How are we to think about this kind of asceticism that comes unannounced and unanticipated, but is likely the primary locus for self-sacrifice? I present three examples: (1) confronting illusion; (2) illness, aging and death; (3) parenting.

Confronting Illusion

Most of us think we see our lives with 20/20 vision. But, chances are, we don't. Some illusions are inherited from culture, nation or family. We see ourselves as better, richer, more generous or more intelligent than others. On the other hand, we may wrongly think that we are not worth much or incapable of holiness. At times we need illusions to function as defense mechanisms that protect us from facing the need to change. We may have illusions about ourselves, our children, jobs, friends, church, even God. Whether we judge ourselves better or worse than what is truly the case, it is risky to build a spiritual life on such a flawed assessment.

In general, we like our illusions. They are familiar and comfortable, and we cling to them even when they drain us of spiritual life. We close our eyes when the truth intrudes on our picture, and we rarely seek outside perspectives from persons who might see us more clearly than we do. Responses from other people that make us especially upset or angry can alert us to some part of the truth about ourselves that we are not willing to face.

An asceticism of everyday life encourages us to desire the truth of our situation. We become willing to be stripped as the layers of illusion are peeled away. We live on the watch for clues to the false dimensions of our lives. Conversations with women reveal that illusions might include the following: Unrestricted generosity is always good. My identity is located exclusively in what others think, want and need. I am not very smart. I could never learn to change a tire or invest money in the stock market. I could never be comfortable eating out, traveling or going to a museum by myself. Men are better vehicles of God's revelation than women.

Such asceticism may mean watching attentively for signals that others send about our true identity (gifts and faults) or discovering blocks we set up to avoid the truth about ourselves and our world. We may have a gift for creating community in a family, neighborhood or business, but shy away from the responsibility that exercising this gift entails. Those who have children, loving spouses or good friends are at an advantage. Those who truly love us play a role in keeping us honest. Children are merciless about perceived failings in parents: the toddler who regales the first grade with an account of a marital spat or the teenager who views parents primarily as annoying, embarrassing style-crampers. Not hard to keep humility in place with this crew around.

More gentle challenges to our illusions may come from loving spouses, partners, friends or colleagues. But we may be left to other devices. Practices include keeping a journal in which we practice honesty with ourselves; seeking information from those close to us; or confiding in a spiritual director we respect and trust. Finally, the asceticism of confronting illusion does not apply only to individuals. It may involve getting at the truth of a local or global political situation, a family, neighborhood or church, and following through with some action. This aspect of the spiritual life usually entails pain and suffering, but it has the potential to lead to new life and the truth that will make us free (see John 8:31–38).

Illness, Aging and Death

A second example of everyday asceticism involves the experiences of illness, aging and death. Often this opportunity for asceticism first knocks in middle age—but not always. Energy levels and body functions begin to decline. We discover we need glasses, then our knees start to hurt. We get tired more quickly, and thus, cannot do as much—likely just when we are called upon to care for elderly parents as well as children. Younger people assume positions of influence and leadership—we are no longer the "expert" others consult. In later life, friends and family may succumb to serious illness and die—conversation turns to surgeries and hospital stays. We may live in denial, or cling ferociously to youth. But Christian spirituality offers an alternative in which physical diminishment, and the mental strain that can accompany it, are part of a larger picture. Suffering and limitation become channels for participation in the suffering of the world and in Christ's sufferings—gestures of acceptance that nurture love and life in ourselves and others.

This stripping intensifies when death approaches. For the elderly and seriously ill, the stripping can be intense—physical movement, eyesight, hearing, memory—even speech, slip out of one's control. How vulnerable we become! And yet these trials provide an opportunity to open ourselves ever more fully to the loving presence and care of God. The discipline of fasting pales in the light of this invitation to lay down one's life with courage and love.

Loved ones of the sick and elderly experience their own brand of asceticism. How do we deal with the fatigue and burnout of daily hospital visits? How do we manage to keep up the daily round of responsibilities that do not abate because someone in the family is ill or dying? How do we allow God to share the burden of grief and of letting go when a friend, child, spouse or parent dies? The weight of such experiences can crush us, or it can be seen as a call to lay down our lives in love, and emerge as persons fully alive in the Spirit.

Seeing life's suffering through a Christian lens helps us avoid stoic resignation, despair or giving up. Instead it links us to Christ and the world on the cross. Embracing trials as avenues to intimacy with God does not support the idea that suffering is good for us. On the contrary, suffering is to be alleviated at every turn. We are called to work tirelessly to eliminate suffering, including the innocent suffering of war, greed, famine, poverty and the tearing of our social fabric. Yet Christ invites us to see these stripping experiences as sacred pieces of the mosaic of our journey to holiness.

In the past, we may have looked too exclusively to unusual ascetic models and have failed to see the heroism all around us. Even a visionary person such as Thomas Merton, a Trappist monk of Gethsemane, can on occasion miss the more ordinary examples of everyday asceticism. In a short piece in *The New Yorker*, Marvin Barrett offers a vivid description of the trauma of heart attack and cancer, and of life in the intensive care unit. He notes that Merton writes about the marginal man, the monk, the displaced person, the prisoner and those who live in the presence of death and go beyond it to witness to life. He wonders why Merton leaves the other experts off his list—the elderly, the desperately ill?

Parenting
A final example of the asceticism of everyday life is experienced by a great number of people—raising children. Perhaps the challenge of raising children is the ascetic opportunity *par excellence*. I do not mean to deny the profound joys and rewards of parenting—the unexpected gesture of love and gratitude—from a simple flower to a homemade birthday card; participating in the process of a child's maturation; helping them become loving persons; witnessing their accomplishments and their growth in learning and self-reflection.

But whether we have children of our own or help others who are raising children, we are daunted by the minefield facing parents today. How do we love children well? How do we allow them to become who they are meant to be, free from our excessive attempts to mold them into something else? How do we learn to trust them and lead them to trust? How do we let them know how much God loves them? How do we expose and invite them to values, to the riches of the tradition? How do we cope with alcohol, drugs, misuse of sexuality, indifference, selfishness, boredom and consumerism? How do we let them go gracefully and lovingly when the time comes?

Parents get a lot of bad press in the media. Films portray parents as confused and out of it. In contrast, youth see life clearly, assess it accurately and act to win the day. This is unfortunate, because most parents know more than their children, desire to love them well and suffer untold agonies in the process. Childrearing is almost always an exercise in failure as well as success—an invitation to heroic asceticism.

It is not hard to find concrete examples, illustrative of the daily round of self-sacrifice that is the lot of most parents. Who does not recognize the rigors of providing transportation to school, doctors' appointments, soccer games, piano lessons, science fairs? Couples who are both employed face hard decisions about child care. Single working parents are stretched to their limits when children fall ill. And what about those whose budgets do not stretch to pay for medicine or braces, or the needed tools for education? A full night's sleep, time to oneself, the freedom to come and go as one pleases—all this must be given up, and given up in a way that is quite different from the monk who chooses to rise during the night to recite his prayers. Being present to children often extends to the second and even third generation, with grandparents and great-grandparents continuing to be deeply involved in the lives of their families.

This vision of "Lent comes to you" asceticism is overtly communal in its orientation. While authentic, private, ascetic practices redound to the welfare of the broader community, a true asceticism of everyday life, by its very nature, directly enhances our life *together*. In either case—and the one does not exclude the other—the fruit is the same: tender compassion, freedom, joy, courage and the fullness of life.

A theology of Trinity, creation, incarnation and Holy Spirit demands that we understand asceticism primarily in terms of daily demands and struggles. We become saints *in and through* the joys and trials of living, not in spite of them. We are invited to reflect on our suffering and sacrifice in light of the cross, the symbol of God's love for humanity.

What a shame if we miss these daily invitations to heroic asceticism, self-denial, the free and loving surrender of life for another. Choosing to fast periodically is laudable, but this is not the primary way to lay down our lives for others. "[A]s you did to the least of these who are members of my family, you did to me" (Matthew 25:40). The spiritual life is a journey into the fullness of life and love in God and one another. Ascetic practice is one means to this end.

It is time for the Christian community to make a paradigmatic shift of images. The model of the monk is only one—and not the primary—model of asceticism for the Christian community. Women and men who struggle to live in the truth, face illness and aging with courage and grace and die to self in parenting, are models for all of us. As women of the church, we are called to the love embodied in daily asceticism. This avenue to fresh vision and new life becomes another way to participate in the divine life. We acknowledge and celebrate the grassroots holiness that surrounds us. We celebrate the presence of God amidst life's suffering. We rejoice, affirm, encourage and console one another.

Afterword: Asceticism Is Not...!

Any conversation about asceticism is incomplete without a word about beauty and pleasure.[14] A wrongheaded concept of asceticism suppresses beauty by focusing only on harsh self-denial. We may erroneously think that if we are having a good time, we could not possibly be on a track toward sainthood. If it does not hurt, it must not please God or be good for us. God is imagined as a dour, stingy replica of Dr. Seuss's *The Grinch Who Stole Christmas*. We may have the idea that if we want to be religious or spiritual, there is no place for pleasure, emotional satisfaction or happiness—suspect enjoyments that can be safely enjoyed only in heaven.

Theology or faith without beauty is a grim prospect indeed. As much as we need to see everyday asceticism as part of our spirituality, so too pleasure and beauty are irreplaceable paths to holiness. A good friend tells a story about a treasured memory—a conversation with her priest the night before her wedding. He told her that she should bring to the communion table on Sunday what she shared with her spouse on her wedding night. It is unfortunate when religion misses this point and errs by thinking about beauty in narrow, opposing terms—shallow or trivial on the one hand, self-indulgent on the other. We are wrong to exclude beauty from our experience and talk about God. When a culture (or a church) gets confused about the differences between genuine beauty and pseudo-beauty, it is easy to throw out the baby with the bathwater. We live in such a culture. Self-centered pleasures include amassing things or attributing professional success, physical health or even inner peace to our efforts alone. We covet designer gowns, hairstyles and the automobiles of the rich and famous. The omnipresence of pseudo-beauty and pseudo-pleasure—the superficially pretty and assembly line creativity—may lead Christians to be wary of any beauty, preventing us from seeking its true forms.

Each of us experiences beauty's pleasure in different ways. Our initial discussion about the meaning of theology included an experience of beauty—the Grand Canyon. But whether our ideas of beauty and pleasure are drawn from nature, relationships, our bodies, our families, music, prayer, sports, architecture, dance or simply a good hot dog at a baseball game, they can have a central role in our spiritual lives. As we grow in our sensitivity to beauty, we get a tiny glimpse of who God might be, for God is Beauty and Pleasure. Humans are aware of their enjoyment of God's creation. Sacramental consciousness stems from our conviction that the world is a reflection of God. We can also rejoice that God takes pleasure in our enjoyment of beauty as a divine gift.

In the spiritual life, the broader canvas for beauty includes the practice of the virtues. To live as we are meant to live—made in God's image and invited into God's presence—is a beautiful thing to be enjoyed and celebrated. How often do we perceive a life marked by kindness, patience, compassion, humor, righteous anger, peace or courage as something of exquisite beauty? Not only are we beautiful when we are good, but being good engenders a deeper sensitivity to beauty in all its forms. This ethical idea of beauty is the larger context in which we take pleasure in a child's first step, a candlelit dinner, the first bud of spring, the call of the mourning dove, a perfectly calculated equation, a Bach fugue, a first glance of a mountain peak covered with snow.

Learning how to take pleasure in the large and small things of life is part of learning how to become a saint. This skill allows our sense of awe and wonder to blossom. Every authentic spiritual life contains an element of "Wow!" And from wonder springs gratitude. To live life as "Thank you" rather than as "You owe me" spares us the inevitable anger and resentment when the world fails to deliver what we demanded. The world does not "owe" us anything. The world is a gift of God.

Thomas Merton and David Steindl-Rast often spoke of gratitude as the heart and foundation of a contemplative existence. On the way to gratitude, we encounter beauty, pleasure, joy and contemplation. In imitation of God, we learn to take pleasure in the world's beauty and in being good. God cannot but enjoy us when we are good—and we trust that God's love endures even when we are not good. We are invited, lured, challenged to become part of this divine joy. The beauty and goodness we see in creation echoes in our virtuous behaviors; the goodness of our lives makes us ever more alert and sensitive to the beauties and goodness in the world.

Discerning the difference between hedonistic pleasure and real joy is crucial. The first is only about me. The second includes the whole world and God. The love of God transforms unholy desires into holy ones. Enjoyment of sexual expression or the opportunity to visit Niagara Falls or the Louvre can be routine or selfish, or it can be an integral part of life with God. Everyday pleasures are part of our spiritualities when we dwell in the awareness of God's generous love. This does not mean that we think about God all day. But when we stand back to reflect, pray and do theology, we strive to renew our desire that the overarching orientation of life tends toward God and empathetic compassion for others.

The spiritual life can never include the suppression of pleasure. True joy confronts excessive Christian rigor and legalism, as well as empty, egotistical satisfactions. When life involves noticing and responding to the vulnerable, needy yet beautiful lives of others, it becomes a joyful existence. The life of faith becomes ever more pleasurable because the simple joys of daily life are no longer primarily the fruit of clinging attachments and addictions but of a loving and free responsibility for the world. Embracing the beauty of the world's mystery and unexplained depths is cause for rejoicing...how could this *not* be God's will for us?

FOOD FOR THOUGHT

1. Identify one compulsion in your life (any form of perfectionism at work or home, shopping at certain stores or buying certain brands, alcohol, exercise). Devise an ascetic practice (do it for at least one month) that will enable you to disrupt this behavior. Keep track of any changes in your ideas, sense of self and others, your experience of being free.

2. Reflect on the differences between a chosen practice or mandated ascetic act (Catholics used to be known for eating fish on Fridays and giving up candy for Lent), and one that has been brought into your life unbidden. How do you see them relating to each other?

3. Give one example of an experience in which "Lent came to you." How do you connect this trial with growth in holiness and nearness to God?

4. Identify some activities, experiences, relationships, accomplishments that bring you the most pleasure in life. In what ways do you connect joy, happiness, fulfillment and pleasure with God and the development of your spiritual life?

5. How do you transmit an appreciation for natural, artistic and virtuous beauty to your daughters (family, friends)?

CHAPTER NINE

• "THE VIRTUOUS WOMAN": NEW WINE IN NEW WINESKINS •

Virtue ethics is an aspect of theology that has direct connections with our spiritualities. Virtue—one of the many theological ways to speak about holiness—has to do with attitudes and behaviors that bring good to the individual and the community. The Latin term *virtus* means "strength," in this case, spiritual strength. Building on the philosophy of Aristotle, Thomas Aquinas wrote that a lifetime of good acts ends up turning us into good persons. Good or bad behavior, repeated over extended periods of time, affects our very identity.

Over time, the community identifies admired qualities and holds up as models individuals who exemplify these virtues. Virtue is a way to talk about what is most truly human in us—love, peace, kindness, courage. No aspect of our lives is off limits to grace. And just as we cannot relegate theology to professional theologians, we cannot relegate holiness to monks and nuns. The call to the virtuous life is universal, grounded in baptism. We all have a responsibility to call each other forth in our journeys toward holiness.

Since the community's ideas about virtue are based primarily upon male experience, it is pressing for women to voice their experience of virtue. What language and imagery do women choose to describe virtue in their lives? What obstacles do they encounter? What misunderstandings need clarification? How do women support each other in the practice of virtue? Traditional understandings of virtue may not transfer easily to women's experience. Men and women are enculturated in different ways and this affects how we live out our spiritualities.

For example, we have defined pride in a way that is foreign to many women—arrogance, excessive self-confidence, an overreaching sense of self that makes us deny God's role in our lives. As a consequence, women may be oblivious to the way pride actually does operate in their lives. Are our children virtually the *best* children in the world? Do we feel superior because we are generous or choose to work behind the scenes? Often sin lurks in those areas of life in which we have special gifts—an example of this is the virtue of generosity treated below. In these cases, what looks on the surface like virtue may, upon closer inspection, turn out to be false or pseudo-virtue.

In order to make this point more concretely, I have identified four virtues that I think are crucial for women's spirituality. They are generosity, courage/risk, humility and hope.

Generosity

Church and society have assigned to women the virtue of generosity in a particular way. All of us would admit that generosity is an important virtue in any community. Imagine life without it. We know and appreciate women who possess this virtue. But a closer examination reveals that generosity is a virtue that can become deeply problematic for women's moral and spiritual development. Since generosity almost always looks attractive on the surface, it can be difficult to notice its potential dark side for women.

The constant exhortation to be generous, with its many rewards, can lead some women to become deeply identified with it. Being a generous person then becomes a vested interest to be protected at all costs. Women are conditioned in overt and subtle ways to place generosity at the heart of what it means to be a "good wife," "a good mother," "a good colleague," "a good friend." To suggest to a woman that she is selfish is usually received as a serious insult. The deeper, more probing question about being generous is this: Are we choosing this behavior *in freedom?*

All motivations are mixed. We are generous because people need help; because we love others; because society and church expect women to be generous; because maintaining our identity requires it; because it makes us feel good. But unless there is a growing sense of freedom, the end result is guaranteed to be anger and resentment.

There are other unfavorable effects of a generosity that is not free. We may become so dependent on "doing for others" that we lose the ability to offer genuine generosity to ourselves. Second, pseudo-generosity can become a camouflage for my real identity. I may become addicted to this virtue because of the way it reinforces an image of myself that I like, but may not be true. I am so busy *needing* to please others that I miss out on who I really am in God's eyes. Third, recipients of pseudo-generosity sense that they are being manipulated, thus alienating women from the very persons they love most.

On the surface, pseudo-generosity appears to be in the interest of the receiver, but at its heart, it is not. Consider the case of Sue who went out of her way to invite her teenage son's friends to their house. She bought a pool table, provided the most popular snacks, and gave them the run of the house. Everyone thought she was the best Mom in the neighborhood. Her approach seemed reasonable, given the dangers young people face in today's culture. But when she looked closer, Sue discovered that what was at stake was not primarily her son's well-being, but her desire for inordinate control. She desperately needed to know about his every move and would go to great lengths to make sure she did.

Recipients of generous acts, whether family members or friends, may feel confused by the clash of motives behind the generosity offered them. Because the social and ecclesial expectation that women be generous is so strong (and in many cases has been interiorized by women), it is easy to be generous out of self-interest or self-image. A final negative effect of this false virtue is resentment, bitterness and anger. Many women in midlife lament that they gave and gave and gave, and no one gave back or said thank you. This is a dangerous outcome that results from our misunderstanding of the anatomy and motives of virtue. The task is to discern good from pseudo-generosity; say no when we suspect marginal motives; and practice developing a love that is free.

Courage/Risk

A second important virtue for women is courage and the risk-taking it requires. We live in an era in which new ideas, new perspectives and new opportunities for women abound. But new thoughts, attitudes and behaviors do not come without struggle and risk. The prophets are models—persons who place themselves clearly and unabashedly on the side of the oppressed, willing to wager their settled world and peace of mind so that something better can emerge. Biblical women provide models—Eve, Hagar, Rebecca, Rachel, Esther, Miriam, Ruth, Mary of Nazareth, Mary Magdalene, Mary and Martha, Phoebe, Lydia. Each took some risk and dealt with the consequences, trusted, reached out to others and worked energetically to realize the kingdom of God.

Along with power, courage is a virtue culturally associated with men, particularly men at war. In the Christian tradition, women who are noted for their spiritual strength (such as martyrs and mystics) often assume or are given a male identity. They are portrayed as soldiers in the battle against evil. As we move into the twenty-first century, it is time to reflect upon the distinctive contours of female courage. What does it look like? In what settings is it expressed? How does it feel? How should we speak of it? Cultivate it?

Like all the virtues, courage is a gift. It is the ability to affirm life in the face of death or non-being. When women experience marginalization in family, society or church, or when they witness the imposition of invisibility on others, it is time to take a deep breath and muster the courage to stand up, speak out and challenge the status quo. Speaking up is doubly difficult for persons who have been consistently rendered voiceless. What prevents us from being risk-takers? We may fear not being liked or being excluded by family or friends who disagree with us. Women are socially conditioned to be peacemakers and yet prophets almost always create trouble. Their actions may result in real physical danger or even death. With the cross as a central Christian symbol, we should be asking ourselves what is wrong if we are *not* in some kind of trouble. Standing up for the truth, for the poor, for the outsider or the abused always exacts a price.

In any worthwhile but difficult endeavor, it is easy to get tired of the hassles, the defeats, the debates—at times even the ridicule—that accompany taking our full place in the community. Many women feel isolated, without the support necessary to stick it out. Other women are timid, not used to taking risks that potentially put them in harm's way. Responsibility for dependents adds yet another level of complexity. Women who have been in dependent patterns of relationship struggle to be with others in mutual and interdependent ways. For women whose lives have been limited to the private sphere, it can be terrifying to confront destructive customs at home or to enter the public arena. Women in the marketplace face challenges that may be directly related to gender.

Whatever it takes for women to embrace their full humanity— which for Christians is living out the truth that we are made in God's image and likeness—requires courage and involves risk. Courage can be public and social or quiet and behind the scenes. One size does not fit all. Each of us must decide for herself. Responding to the grace of prophecy will be unique for every woman in her specific circumstances. Each day is filled with small and great opportunities to exercise courage but it takes sustained, conscious attention and practice: Speaking up when jokes are made at another's expense, finding ways to include the poor, immigrants or persons of color; walking in the shoes of another; or engaging our imaginations help us address professional competitive situations in which women pit themselves against other women; or, we can just hang tight when our children plead for clothing, music, games and activities that denigrate women.

Courage is linked with the vitality and power of life. It is the power to create beyond oneself without losing oneself. Courage is a crucial element in the gospel call to envision a new heaven and a new earth. As women, we are called to attend to the distinctive contours of this life force within. How do we experience the power of courage? In what particular situations are we being summoned to speak the prophetic word? Courageous women who voice a new vision of the Christian life are models for the entire church.

Humility

"Make us humble, Lord…but not now." When you read the works of the mystics—male or female—the virtue of humility is superseded in importance only by charity. Humility has traditionally been at the center of the Christian understanding of holiness. It was important because it offset the vice of pride, which was seen as the most serious of sins. Pride is said to be the sin behind the first transgression by Adam and Eve, and the human race has been suffering ever since. Humility was also valued because it was linked to the life and witness of Jesus who was humble even to death on a cross. Christianity is constructed on the paradox that life emerges out of death; the humble shall be exalted (see Matthew 23:11–12; Luke 1:52); the last shall be first (see Luke 13:29–30); to lose one's life is to find it. Many stories in the New Testament attest to this paradox. Jesus counsels people not to take the seats of honor at a party but rather to choose the lowest seat so the host can say "Friend, go up higher" (Luke 14:7–11). The root of the word *humility* is from the Latin term for "earth" or "soil" *(humus)*. The expression "down to earth," captures one aspect of this virtue.

Humility is such a profound virtue that you cannot approach it directly. To set out to be humble is already not to be. Humility is also a stumbling block in cultures that run on a "me-first" principle. Cynics remind us that humility does not pay. If I don't put myself forward, someone else will get the prize and I will end up at the bottom of the social barrel. Women are particularly sensitive to the ways in which humility has been used to keep them silent, to bar them from power or to keep them in violent, abusive situations (see 1 Timothy 2:9–15; Titus 2:3–5). We all know the damning phrase "uppity woman" used by men, but more often by women who are threatened by women who live outside "acceptable" female boundaries. Psychological studies demonstrate that many women lack confidence in themselves and their abilities. The media bombards women with messages that they are not smart enough, strong enough, logical enough or moral enough to compete in a male-dominated world. Television commercials continue to offer demeaning images of women (men do not escape either). Humility can thus be seen to work against female development, blocking self-confidence, self-assertion, self-realization. But our enemy is not genuine humility but the pseudo-humility that arises from misunderstanding this virtue.

Let us explore first what humility is not and then take a further look at what it is. Humility does not mean having a low opinion of oneself. It does not require rejection or self-hatred or lack of assertiveness. Humility does not mean neglecting to develop gifts or allowing ourselves to become doormats. Nor should we confuse humility with humiliation. To be humble is to live in the truth; to be humiliated is to allow insults or setbacks to wound our self-image. The humble are not necessarily silent or invisible. In fact, a person who makes a point of being self-effacing and "humble" and then gloats over being holier than others is guilty of the sin of pride, not a practitioner of the virtue of humility.

What then is humility? It has to do with the *truth* about oneself and the world. We don't decide to be humble, but our spiritualities can prepare us to be receptive to this virtue. The humble person acknowledges and uses her gifts with simplicity and gratitude. Honesty about sinfulness brings compunction and the desire to seek and receive forgiveness. Humility can be found in anyone, but it is often the fruit of a long life, lived in openness to God's grace.

Humility also grows when we notice the awesome, infinite love and generosity of God, and see ourselves as small and insignificant in comparison. I envy physicists and astronomers who study the vast magnificence of the universe. They know firsthand what it is to feel small and insignificant. In a very deep sense, this perspective is simply true. In light of God's greatness, humility involves accepting our status as creatures, knowing that we are sinful, and welcoming our gifts with gratitude. Catherine of Siena says to God, "You are Everything. I am nothing."[15] When it is real, seeing oneself as nothing does not diminish the parallel truth that we are made in God's image. It emerges out of the truth that God is great and life is a gift.

Reason and psychological knowledge are key resources to help us discover our true selves. Humility adds another dimension—ultimately it is the fruit of openness to God's generous love and mystery. To be humble is to be free of pretense, to be able to forgive and be forgiven, to have oneself in perspective in order to resist exaggeration of either one's gifts or one's faults. True Christian humility does not involve denying our own dignity. Rather it is a working toward recognition of our true achievements and faults—that is, learning to see ourselves truly as God sees us. Saint Benedict taught that humility is for the strong. It is a sign of maturity in the faith to be no longer childishly dependent, but responsible to work with God in service to others.

In our discussion on confronting illusion, we called attention to the importance of community. Perhaps the most important human source of truth about ourselves is each other. We are our sisters' keepers and we need each other to become saints. God has bestowed on us both the privilege and the responsibility to help each other discover who we truly are in the sight of God. Too often, women are other women's worst enemies. We are threatened by women who are different from us, or in competition with us. The humble tend to focus on their own sins rather than the sins of others. Humility leads us to refrain from judgment and to be more patient and tolerant of the foibles of others, because we are so clear about our own.

The model for humble living is Jesus Christ, who refused to cling to divine status (see Philippians 2:5–9); possessed a deep reverence for and patience with others; reflected an interior silence and self-possession; and was willing to forgive. Jesus is the antithesis of arrogance and self-preoccupation. He cared about the poor; washed the feet of his disciples (see John 13:3); forgave those who crucified him. Spiritual disciplines prepare us to receive the gift of humility. To practice humility is to assume a countercultural stance against a status quo that encourages arrogance and self-aggrandizement at the expense of others (see Romans 12:16). In a world rife with conflict, humility points the way to forgiveness and reconciliation.

Walking in the way of humility is a task of a lifetime. Given a tradition that is at best ambiguous toward women, our practice of humility can be complex and tricky. It is like walking a tightrope. We cannot allow pseudo-humility to undermine our humanity but it seems unwise to reject this virtue altogether. Humility involves a profound mystery in which we see ourselves, our families and our nations simultaneously as glorious and graced on the one hand, and as unexceptional, and even downright sinful on the other. Humility is learned when we discover the simple truth of existence by living faithful lives of love and remaining open to grace. Humility knows the gifts and miseries of others, responds in compassion and does great things because our surety is in God. "Take my yoke upon you, and learn from me; for I am gentle and humble in heart, and you will find rest for your souls" (Matthew 11:29).

Hope

The conflicts and devastation reported on the evening news test our hope. And yet genuine Christian hope is grounded in the conviction that God's grace will prevail, not only at the end of history, but now, within it. Embedded in hope is the ability (ultimately the gift) to imagine a future characterized by love, dignity and mutual respect among all persons, including all women, the confidence that such a reality is possible and the conviction to work tirelessly to bring it about. In one of Charles Péguy's poems God voices an ease in understanding faith and love but sees hope as a wonder, a miracle, a mystery, an unexpected sight.[16]

Genuine hope is different from the surface optimism expressed when we say we hope it will not rain tomorrow. It may or may not ground our comforting words to our children that "everything will be all right." Our deepest hope emerges in limited situations, in times of trial, darkness, illness, war and exile. Hope shows up when negative human experiences make fullness of life seem impossible, unreachable, beyond our grasp. Hope is our response to darkness. It is that strange mysterious light that illumines the abyss. Hope is born of the conviction that God's love cannot fail. It is behind fourteenth-century anchoress Julian of Norwich's famous line, "All will be well."

In the history of civilization, including Christianity, women have known unfathomable darkness. For the most part, women's existence, thoughts, creativity, actions, writings and goodness were ignored, diminished and destroyed. The voices of so many women burned at the stake as witches as well as pioneer women driven to insanity in the drive westward, remain silent. We need periodically to engage in rituals in which we lament and weep over symphonies not written, poetry not penned, sermons not preached, countries not governed, businesses not developed, stories not told, because of women's devaluation. But in spite of this lamentable past, and against great odds, women hoped, thought, wrote, created, sang, prayed, worked, raised families and became saints.

Women's struggle for freedom and dignity reveals many faces of hope. Our hope is nurtured by the ongoing discovery of women's truth; by women's solidarity with each other; by examples of mutual cooperation with supportive men; by gradual changes in church and society that acknowledge and use women's gifts. Hope is a virtue that can become a way of life. It allows us to create the future with quiet confidence and joy, even when things don't go our way. When we are tempted to diminish our efforts, hope provides energy to keep at it in ever more thoughtful and creative ways. Hope stems from an inner freedom that is modeled by the saints both living and dead. Its source is in their communion with God, the reservoir and promise of final victory. The saints claim certitude because, in a real sense, they see with God's eyes.

Those who are the bearers of this extraordinary virtue of hope are important to the entire community. Each time we encounter a woman of hope and joy, we find our own hope renewed, our imagination and commitment rekindled. Hope prods us to step out again, to imagine, to speak, to risk, to put ourselves on the line, to dare to work toward the kingdom—together. Paul captures one aspect of the struggle: "I consider that the sufferings of this present time are not worth comparing with the glory about to be revealed to us" (Romans 8:18). But even more relevant is the truth that this eschatological vision of heaven is also meant to be realized in the present. The vision includes women and men working together in respectful mutuality for the good of women, all peoples and the world.

FOOD FOR THOUGHT

1. Make a list of persons you know and admire whom you consider spiritually strong or virtuous. Name one or two virtues they possess that you would like to develop in your own life.

2. How do you react to the term *humility?* Discuss some of the dangers for women of misunderstanding and misusing this virtue.

3. Spiritual disciplines help us grow in virtue. Identify a virtue you would like to develop. Then begin each day with a short prayer asking God to help you exercise this virtue (for example, speaking up instead of being timid about voicing your thoughts). At the end of each day, reflect on when you did or did not practice this virtue and ask for the grace to persevere in this process of spiritual growth.

RITUAL

- *Centering exercise.* Take a moment to breathe deeply and slowly. Pay attention to your breath. Inhale slowly for a count of five. Hold for a count of five. Exhale slowly for a count of ten. Repeat this exercise about five times. Imagine stress, worry and anxiety flowing out of your body as you exhale. Imagine the healing power of the Spirit being drawn into you as you inhale.
- *Reflect.* Bring to mind a woman in your life or a woman in the world who embodies for you the best qualities of the virtue of humility. In your imagination, have a short, honest conversation with her about this virtue.
- *Write.* On a small piece of paper, jot down a false understanding of humility that you want to reject or eliminate from your life. Exchange papers with the person next to you and slowly rip up the paper (if you are alone, simply rip up your own paper) and place the pieces in a bowl in the center of the group.
- *Read.* Do a slow, dramatic reading of the Magnificat (Luke 1:46–55).
- *Pray.* With this image of Mary before you, voice a prayer of desire, hope, gratitude or celebration related to this virtue among women.

CHAPTER TEN

• THEOLOGY AND SPIRITUALITY AS PARTNERS •

There is growing concern about widespread ignorance of the Christian tradition in the West. In *Religious Literacy: What Every American Needs to Know—And Doesn't,* Stephen Prothero laments what he calls loss of religious memory. It is both enlightening and discouraging to learn about all the forces leading to our inability to identify Abraham or Moses, locate the phrase, "Blessed are the poor in spirit" among the beatitudes, name Jesus' birthplace (many answer Jerusalem), or list the four Gospels accurately. Ten percent of Americans think that Joan of Arc was Noah's wife! The need to learn about the theology and spirituality of our Christian ancestors is acute.

It is my hope that reading this book will awaken your desire to learn more about the Christian tradition. Study is a necessary first step before we can critically appropriate the tradition for today. Books, tapes, workshops, adult education courses that present the history and content of the faith in an ordered, disciplined way are crucial to doing grassroots theology. The pattern of an elite corps of informed Christians and large numbers of uninformed laity is no longer acceptable. All of us need these tools to interpret our faith and enter into dialogue with our contemporary world. Theology informed by love—also known as wisdom —is the birthright of all the baptized.

We conclude our conversations by returning to how theology and spirituality might support, enrich and correct each other. Spirituality is what faith looks like in the way we live each day of our lives. It has to do with the ordinary (or at times extraordinary) attitudes, dispositions, choices, behaviors and relationships that life presents to each of us. Good theology draws believers into deeper spiritual engagement through its formulations of the doctrines of the Trinity, Christ and the Holy Spirit. For example, spirituality notices the beauty of oceans, mountains and ladybugs and intones a prayer of thanksgiving. Theology describes God as a generous, creative giver of gifts. Spirituality contributes to efforts against torture or helps build a new house in the inner city. Theology examines the meaning of sin and redemption. Let us begin our conversation about this relationship by listing some of the ways in which theology helps spirituality.

Theology's Gifts to Spirituality

To begin, theology slows us down. It counsels us to reflect on what we are doing in our spiritual lives and why. Theology asks: What has our spirituality to do with the Bible and religious tradition? What language best describes our experience of God? Our culture values spontaneity and informality—important values that should be part of all spiritualities —but theology reminds spirituality that the unreflected life is not worth living. Good theology can save spirituality from mindless, chaotic enthusiasm, wrong turns or anemia. It wards off the chaos that can ensue when religious experience has no bounds, no order and no criteria for authenticity.

We may be drawn to a spirituality focused on gardening, or one that involves crystals or aromatherapy. Theology's job is not to judge new spiritual practices prematurely, but to probe, ask critical questions and test their legitimacy in light of the Christian story. Theology helps us live our spiritual lives intelligently, making decisions that are based on the hard-won wisdom of the ages. Theology can also assist us in discerning and defending genuine prophetic and charismatic expressions from phony ones.

We may not think language is important but, in fact, it has great influence on how we perceive the world and act. One of theology's jobs is to help us be more precise in the way we talk about the faith as it evolves through time. Over the centuries, church councils have debated and made decisions about the content of the faith. For example, we speak of Jesus as true God and true man. This language guards against spiritual movements that overemphasize the divinity of Christ or movements that do the reverse, seeing Christ only in his humanity and ignoring his divinity.

In addition, it is theology's job to discern to what extent new spiritual ideas and practices embody gospel values and tradition. As each generation develops and changes, spiritual practices adapt to the new context. A culture with a keen interest in physical health will have many people running, walking, biking, playing sports. Some will use this time and the experience of physical exercise to pray, to be mindful of God's gifts in endowing the human person with such skills. Theology will remind joggers that being fit is a way to honor our bodies and spirits, which are made in God's image. It helps hikers notice the difference between being fit so I can be the best-looking gal on the block and being fit so that I am better prepared to praise God and serve others in Christ's name.

Theology also reminds spirituality that the Christian life is not about "me and God" in a narrow, individualistic sense. While I may shape my spiritual practices in the light of my one, short lifetime and the cultural trends of the moment, Christian theology keeps track of the two thousand years in which Christians in every corner of the globe have lived and struggled to love God and live virtuous lives oriented to others—not to mention comparison with more ancient religions such as Judaism and Hinduism and how they relate to each other. In our culture, it is easy to think (wrongly) that salvation is about me as an individual. Theology reminds us that salvation is a community affair. We go to heaven together or we don't go at all.

Spirituality's Gifts to Theology

If we turn the tables, we discover that spirituality has a lot to offer theology as well. Spirituality keeps theology in touch with the everyday life of faith "on the ground." Spirituality reminds theology that its goal is not only clarity and order but also keeping spiritual traditions alive and thriving. Spirituality prevents theology from turning in on itself, retreating to the ivory towers of academe and producing tomes of deadening, unintelligible language. At times, spirituality may lack adequate order; theology can have too much. Theology should not render invisible the messy, open-ended, uncontrollable aspects of life. Spirituality says to theology: "Don't forget to incorporate the experiences of the mystics, liturgy and prayer. Remember the 'Wow!' experiences of standing at the edge of the Grand Canyon."

Just as theology keeps watch so that spirituality remains faithful to the gospel and tradition, so too spirituality needs to keep theology faithful to the truth of spiritual experience on the ground. The goal of both theology and spirituality is to lead the community of faith to ever-greater love of God and neighbor. Spirituality reminds theology to keep God at the center, to pray, to remain humble. Spirituality helps theology find ways to express the boundary-breaking and cataclysmic effects of encountering the living God. The language of theology should be clear, but theologians should also stretch language to its limits, helping Christians to "catch" the Spirit of God. Since human experience is so vast and diverse, good theology should shimmer with the presence of paradox and mystery. Spirituality says to theology: "Remember the diversity, the pluralism, the ambiguity of the human encounter with God." Theologians should never have to check their religious experience at the door when they do theology.

Spirituality and theology belong together at their very root. We can imagine them like a circle, each feeding the other in a reciprocal flow. Each has a distinct vocation, but each enriches and is accountable to the other. At times it can be a struggle to keep poetry and doctrine together, but struggle we must. Spirituality is the context, horizon and atmosphere in which theology is done, affecting its methods and results. Spirituality makes theology possible and is its perfection. The novelty of fresh encounters with the Spirit gives rise to interpretation and argumentation. The ultimate mission of both is to serve church and world by building up the body of Christ and offering hope.

FOOD FOR THOUGHT

1. Discuss your sense of yourself as a theologian before and after you read this book.
2. Are there elements of spirituality—as practiced in our present culture—that you feel are at odds with the Christian tradition as you understand it?
3. Identify two ways in which you relate your spiritual life to theology. Are you satisfied that your spirituality is adequately grounded in theology? Any changes you might wish to make?

This brief exploration of the theological foundations of a spirituality of everyday life has come to an end. I hope the words "I am a theologian" come more easily to your lips and fit more comfortably in your mind and heart. Whatever our lives have been, whatever they will bring, we are empowered as human beings to assign meaning to them. As Christian disciples and grassroots theologians, we are free to see every aspect of our existence as gift of God and invitation to participate in God's Triune life. It may be obvious to link prayer, grace before meals, liturgy, retreats and Bible study to theology and to our spiritual lives. But above all, we are called to link politics, rock concerts, exercise in the gym, meetings in boardrooms, work at a factory, in the kitchen, love in the bedroom, events in the neighborhood, the university, the nation, the world and the cosmos—to theology and spirituality.

As women we work to enhance and correct the theology and spirituality that was born out of male experience by adding to the mix life with God from female perspectives. We probe ways in which women assign meaning to their spiritual lives in all their diversity. The way we think about, interpret and name the elements of Christian life—God, faith, virtue, holiness, Spirit-power and Scripture—needs to reflect all the voices in the Christian community. As women, we are charged with the responsibility and privilege of attending to, reflecting on and articulating our encounters with God and life. We need to honor women's experience of faith as the community has honored male experience of faith in order to create a more inclusive, truthful understanding of theology and the Christian spiritual life.

Discovering who we are as women in God's sight is an amazing journey toward truth and love. Our call is to take God and ourselves seriously and to become humble but confident grassroots theologians. We are invited as women to trust that God's grace and love can make all things new, in spite of the silences, oppression and fear that are a significant part of our heritage. Every woman who hopes becomes a beacon to other women and to the world. Julian of Norwich reminds us that Christ never said following him would be easy. What he did say is that we would not be overcome.

• READING THE BIBLE •

The Old Testament was written from approximately 1400 BCE to approximately 400 BCE, primarily in Hebrew, with a few small sections written in Aramaic (a dialect of Hebrew) or Greek. For a summary of the books of the Hebrew Bible, consult Timothy Schehr's *The Bible Made Easy* (St. Anthony Messenger Press, 2007) or another reader friendly introduction.

Hebrew Scriptures

The first five books of the Bible are called the *Pentateuch* or *Torah* (the Jewish term for "Law"): Genesis, Exodus, Leviticus, Numbers and Deuteronomy.

The next grouping includes the historical texts: Joshua, Judges, Ruth, 1 and 2 Samuel, 1 and 2 Kings, 1 and 2 Chronicles, Ezra, Nehemiah and Esther.

The Wisdom Literature includes Job, Psalms, Proverbs, Ecclesiastes, Ecclesiasticus, Song of Songs and the Book of Wisdom.

The prophetic books are Isaiah, Jeremiah, Ezekiel, Daniel, Hosea, Joel, Amos, Obadiah, Jonah, Micah, Nahum, Habakkuk, Zephaniah, Haggai, Zechariah, Malachi.

New Testament

The New Testament contains four Gospels (Matthew, Mark, Luke and John); history: the Acts of the Apostles (seen as part two of Luke's Gospel); the letters of Paul (Romans to Philemon); other letters (Hebrews to Jude) and prophecy: the book of Revelation. The New Testament was written from approximately 45 to approximately 95 CE. The New Testament was written in Koine Greek (common Greek, the everyday form of the Greek language in the first century CE).

Reading the Bible: Getting Started

Below is a short list of some key passages for anyone who wants to begin the practice of Bible reading. As you become familiar with the location and contents of each book of the Bible, you may want to choose an entire book to read from beginning to end. The Gospel of Mark is the shortest Gospel and a good place to begin. Each Gospel emphasizes specific aspects of Jesus' life and ministry. It is an interesting exercise to note these differences as you read each Gospel in its entirety.

The selections are short to enable you to read the texts slowly and prayerfully. When you are touched, moved, angered, puzzled or excited about something in the text, pause to reflect on it. What moves you about the text? Why? What do you think this passage is trying to tell you about your life at this point in your journey? You may want to keep a small notebook to jot down your thoughts and feelings.

Hebrew Scriptures

Genesis 1 and 2	Two stories of creation
Exodus 7—14	Israel moves from slavery to freedom
Judges 4	Deborah: Female courage and determination
Psalm 8	The dignity and beauty of humanity
Psalm 19	In praise of creation
Psalm 23	The Lord is our Shepherd
Psalm 107	Prayer of gratitude
Ruth	Ruth and Naomi: friendship between women
1 Samuel 17	David and Goliath
Esther 1—8	Esther saves her people
Job 1—3	Why do good people suffer?
Ecclesiastes 3:1–9	A time for everything under the sun

New Testament

Matthew 5—7	The Sermon on the Mount
Matthew 13:1–23	The right kind of soil
Matthew 25:14–30	The Ten Talents
Matthew 25:31–46	Love your neighbor
Mark 8:22—10:52	Discipleship/blindness and Jesus' predictions of his suffering
Luke 2:1–20	Jesus' birth
Luke 2:40–52	Jesus growing up in Nazareth
Luke 24:1–12	The resurrected Jesus appears to the women
John 2:1–11	Water into wine
John 9	The blind see
Acts 2	Come, Holy Spirit
Romans 8	Freedom in the Spirit
1 Corinthians 13	What is love?
Philippians 1	We share in God's grace
James 2:1–12	Rich and poor

1. Frederick Crowe, *Lonergan* (Collegeville, Minn. Liturgical, 1992), p. 48.

2. Mark McIntosh, *Mysteries of Faith* (Cambridge, Mass.: Cowley, 2000).

3. McIntosh, p. 2

4. Andrew Greeley, *The Catholic Imagination* (Berkeley, Calif.: University of California Press, 2000), p. 1.

5. Ellen M. Umansky, ed., *Four Centuries of Jewish Women's Spirituality* (Boston: Beacon, 1992), p. 37.

6. Sister M. Madeleva, C.S.C, *The Four Last Things: Collected Poems* (Notre Dame, Ind.: St. Mary's College, 1986), p. 152.

7. Mary Oliver, From *Gaudium et Spes*, 1, available at www.osjspm.org.

8. Raniero Cantalamessa, *Come, Creator Spirit: Meditations on the "Veni Creator"* (Collegeville, Minn.: Liturgical, 2003), p. 1. Some scholars attribute the text to Rhabanus Maurus (c. 780–856), Abbot of Fulda and later Archbishop of Mainz.

9. G.J. Sirks, "The Cinderella of Theology: The Doctrine of the Holy Spirit," *Harvard Theological Review* 50/2 (1957), pp. 77–89.

10. Kilian McDonnell, "Pneumatological Overview: Trinitarian Guidelines for Speaking About the Holy Spirit," *Proceedings of the Catholic Theological Society of America*, 51 (1996), pp. 190–191.

11. Ronald Rolheiser, *The Holy Longing: The Search for a Christian Spirituality* (New York: Doubleday, 1999), p. 7.

12. Jean-Pierre de Caussade, *The Sacrament of the Present Moment* (San Francisco: HarperSanFrancisco, 1982), p. 101.

13. *The Inclusive Psalms* (Brentwood, Md.: Priests for Equality, 1997), p. 8.

14. This section was inspired by the work of Edward Farley, *Faith and Beauty: A Theological Aesthetic* (Aldershot, U.K.: Ashgate, 2001), pp. 101–113.

15. Catherine of Siena, *The Prayers of Catherine of Siena*, Suzanne Noffke, ed. (Mahwah, N.J.: Paulist, 1983), p. 5

16. Charles Péguy, *The Portal of the Mystery of Hope*, David L. Schindler, Jr., trans. (New York: Continuum, 1996), p. 6.

Books

Beaudoin, Tom. *Consuming Faith: Integrating Who We Are With What We Buy.* Lanham, Md.: Sheed and Ward, 2003.

Brown, Raymond E. *Introduction to the New Testament.* New York: Paulist, 1994.

Carr, Anne E. *Transforming Grace: Christian Tradition and Women's Experience.* San Francisco: HarperSanFrancisco, 1988.

Curran, Charles E., Margaret A. Farley and Richard A. McCormick, eds. *Feminist Ethics and the Catholic Moral Tradition.* New York: Paulist, 1996.

Dillard, Annie. *Pilgrim at Tinker Creek.* New York: Harper, 2007.

Dreyer, Elizabeth A. *Earth Crammed With Heaven: A Spirituality of Everyday Life.* New York: Paulist, 1994.

———. *Holy Power, Holy Presence: Rediscovering Medieval Metaphors for the Holy Spirit.* New York: Paulist, 2007.

———. *Manifestations of Grace.* Collegeville, Minn.: Liturgical, 1990.

———. *Passionate Spirituality: Hildegard of Bingen and Hadewijch of Brabant.* New York: Paulist, 2005.

———. *A Retreat with Catherine of Siena.* Cincinnati: St. Anthony Messenger Press, 1999.

Dyckman, Katherine et al., *The Spiritual Exercises Reclaimed: Uncovering Liberating Possibilities for Women.* New York: Paulist, 2001.

Gaillardetz, Richard R. *Transforming Our Days: Spirituality, Community and Liturgy in a Technological Culture.* New York: Crossroad, 2000.

Gula, Richard M. *The Good Life: Where Morality and Spirituality Converge.* New York: Paulist, 1999.

Häring, Bernard. *The Virtues of An Authentic Life: A Celebration of Spiritual Maturity.* Liguori, Mo.: Liguori, 1997.

Hauser, Richard. *Moving in the Spirit: Becoming A Contemplative in Action.* New York: Paulist, 1986.

Keenan, James F. *Virtues for Ordinary Christians.* Kansas City, Mo.: Sheed and Ward, 1996.

Kinast, Robert L. *Making Faith-Sense: Theological Reflection in Everyday Life.* Collegeville, Minn.: Liturgical, 1999.

Pope John Paul II. *Celebrate 2000!: Reflections on the Holy Spirit.* Ann Arbor, Mich.: Servant, 1997.

Schaupp, Joan P. *Woman: Image of the Holy Spirit.* Bethesda, Md.: International Scholars, 1996.

Steindl-Rast, David. *Gratefulness, the Heart of Prayer: An Approach to Life in Fullness.* New York: Paulist, 1984.

Wolski Conn, Joann, ed. *Women's Spirituality: Resources for Christian Development.* New York: Paulist, 1996.

CD

The companion CD for this series, *Called to Holiness: Spirituality for Catholic Women,* features the series theme song, "We Are Called" by David Haas and works by many well known singers and song writers. It is available from GIA Publications at www.GIAmusic.com or St. Anthony Messenger Press at www.CalledtoHoliness.org.

Madeleva Lectures

The Madeleva Lectures are annual talks presented by Saint Mary's College in Notre Dame, Indiana, in which prominent women theologians discuss the role of women in the church today and the need for a more holistic human approach to spirituality. Some of the lectures more relevant to the issues in this book are listed below.

Carmody, Denise Lardner. *An Ideal Church: A Meditation.* 1999.

Chittister, Joan. *Job's Daughters: Women and Power.* 1990.

Dreyer, Elizabeth A. *Passionate Women: Two Medieval Mystics.* 1989.

Hellwig, Monika K. *Christian Women in a Troubled World.* 1985.

Hilkert, Mary Catherine. *Speaking With Authority: Catherine of Siena and the Voices of Women Today.* 2001.

Hinsdale, Mary Ann. *Women Doing Theology.* 2004.

Johnson, Elizabeth A. *Women, Earth, and Creator Spirit.* 1993.

Leckey, Dolores R. *Women and Creativity.* 1991.

Sowle Cahill, Lisa. *Women and Sexuality.* 1992.

Web Resources

Lectures on women in the church by leading women theologians can be viewed at http://data.fairfield.edu/itunesu/.

Please visit our series web site at www.CalledtoHoliness.org.

Called to Holiness Series

A groundbreaking eight-volume series on women's spirituality, *Called to Holiness: Spirituality for Catholic Women* will cover the many diverse facets of a woman's interior life and help her discover how God works with her and through her. An ideal resource for a woman seeking to find how God charges the moments of her life—from spirituality itself, to the spirituality of social justice, the spirituality of grieving the loss of a loved one, the creation and nurturing of families, the mentoring of young adult Catholic women, to recognition of the shared wisdom of women in the middle years—this series can be used by individuals or in groups. Far from the cloister or monastery, these books find God in the midst of a woman's everyday life and help her to find and celebrate God's presence day to day and acknowledge her own gifts as an ordinary "theologian." The books can be used independently or together for individual discussion or group faith sharing. Each book will include gathering rituals, reflection questions and annotated bibliographies.

Living a Spirituality of Action
A Woman's Perspective

Joan Mueller

"Own your gifts and use them to make the world a better place," Catholic theologian Joan Mueller writes. In this practical book she provides us with ideas and encouragement to live and act with courage to change the world, even if our actions are sometimes small.

This is a book for all who hear about hungry people living in the park and decide to make sandwiches, who volunteer to teach children to read, who raise money to change systems that provide substandard care to the vulnerable, who can imagine a mothered world. Mueller invites us to discuss and embrace our shared wisdom.

Release: August 2008
Religion — Spirituality
Paper, 112 pp.
Order #B16885
ISBN 978-0-86716-885-3
$11.95

Called to Holiness Publication Schedule

Fall 2008:

• Making Sense of God:
A Woman's Perspective
(Elizabeth A. Dreyer)
ISBN 978-0-86716-884-6

• Grieving With Grace:
A Woman's Perspective
(Dolores R. Leckey)
ISBN 978-0-86716-888-4

• Living a Spirituality of
Action: A Woman's
Perspective (Joan Mueller)
ISBN 978-0-86716-885-3

Spring 2009:

• Embracing Latina
Spirituality: A Woman's
Perspective
(Michelle A. Gonzalez)
ISBN 978-0-86716-886-0

• Awakening to Prayer:
A Woman's Perspective
(Clare Wagner)
ISBN 978-0-86716-892-1

Fall 2009:

• Creating New Life,
Nurturing Families:
A Woman's Perspective
(Sidney Callahan)
ISBN 978-0-86716-893-8

• Weaving Faith and
Experience: A Woman's
Perspective on the Middle
Years (Patricia Cooney
Hathaway)
ISBN 978-0-86716-904-1

• Finding My Voice:
A Young Adult Woman's
Perspective
(Beth M. Knobbe)
ISBN 978-0-86716-894-5

Called to Holiness Companion CD
Musical selections to accompany the gathering rituals for the book series. Order #A9001 **$19.95**

Grieving With Grace
A Woman's Perspective

Dolores R. Leckey

There are many ways in which the course of our daily lives can be altered—illness, change in residence, loss of employment and death of loved ones. These alterations can require dramatic and even subtle changes in our everyday living, limit our options and force us to choose different priorities.

Dolores Leckey knows firsthand that the death of a spouse changes forever the rhythms of life at all levels—body, mind and soul. In this moving and personal narrative that includes entries from her journal, she shares with us her own shift in consciousness, in the way she sees God, herself and the world after her husband's death. She offers us consolation and hope.

Release: August 2008
Religion — Spirituality
Paper, 112 pp.
Order #B16888
ISBN 978-0-86716-888-4
$11.95

ABOUT THE AUTHOR

Elizabeth A. Dreyer is editor of this series and professor of religious studies at Fairfield University in Fairfield, Connecticut. She lectures widely on the Christian tradition, especially medieval mysticism, grace, the Holy Spirit and contemporary lay spirituality. She wrote *Holy Power, Holy Presence: Medieval Metaphors of the Holy Spirit, Passionate Spirituality: Hildegard of Bingen and Hadewijch of Brabant, Earth Crammed With Heaven: A Spirituality of Everyday Life* and *A Retreat with Catherine of Siena: Living the Truth in Love*. With Mark Burrows she edited *Minding the Spirit: The Study of Christian Spirituality*. She lives in Hamden, Connecticut with her husband, John Bennett.